D1155764

Presenting LifeRing Secular Recovery

A Selection of Readings
for Treatment Professionals

LifeRing Press
Oakland, California

Permission to reprint portions of this publication is gratefully acknowledged. An earlier version of this publication was issued in loose-leaf binder format in October 1998. Portions of this edition were previously published on www.unhooked.com, and have been modified for this volume.

LifeRing Secular Recovery, LifeRing Recovery, LifeRing Press, and the lifering logo are registered trademarks of Lifering Inc. LifeRing Inc. is a nonprofit corporation.

For additional copies of this publication, contact:

LifeRing Press
1440 Broadway Suite 1000
Oakland CA 94612-2029

www.lifering.com
books@lifering.com
Tel: 510-793-0779
Fax: 510-763-1513

To arrange for LifeRing speakers to address staff and/or clients, contact LifeRing Secular Recovery Service Center at the same address and phone numbers, or email service@lifering.com

First edition September 2000

10 9 8 7 6 5 4 3 2

ISBN 0-9659429-2-9

Table of Contents

Preface: Presenting LifeRing Secular Recovery

Dear Treatment Professional:

This booklet is an introduction to LifeRing Secular Recovery, a network of self-help support groups that offers a positive supplement to the traditional treatment approaches. LifeRing Recovery groups enhance the client's intrinsic motivation to get clean and sober, stimulate clients to take responsibility for their recovery, and support each client to work up an individualized abstinence program.

Treatment professionals at facilities where LifeRing Recovery meetings have become established, such as the Kaiser Permanente Chemical Dependency Recovery Programs in the San Francisco Bay Area, recommend LifeRing without hesitation. LifeRing S.R. is an uncompromisingly abstinence-based approach. It urges members to make sobriety the number one priority in life, and teaches "Don't Drink Or Use, No Matter What." Although the LifeRing philosophy differs from the 12-Step approaches, LifeRing co-exists peacefully with 12-Step meetings at treatment facilities, and members can if they wish attend both kinds of groups.

One of the most innovative recent referral approaches is to schedule LifeRing meetings side by side with 12-Step meetings on the treatment premises, and require clients to attend the meeting of their choice. In this way, clients can explore both approaches at will, and when they settle on their preference, they will have done so by way of exercising a choice, enhancing their level of commitment.

The treatment program that has secular support groups available for referrals enjoys a broadened spectrum of modalities. Although the traditional programs help many, they were never intended for everyone, and not everyone benefits from them. A program that includes a secular supplement may be able to help clients who would otherwise end up on the minus side of the facility's outcomes profile.

In this booklet you will find letters of reference, a theoretical explanation, a historical perspective, a comparative review, and an account of a clinical protocol with a concept similar to that on which LifeRing is based. I hope that after reading these materials you will include LifeRing S.R. groups on your referral list. LifeRing also maintains an active presence on the World Wide Web, www.unhooked.com, which carries a list of current meetings nationwide. If you have further questions or concerns, please do not hesitate to contact the LifeRing S.R. Service Center to ask for more information or to book a LifeRing speaker.

In sobriety,

Marty N.
For the LifeRing S.R. Service Center

The Permanente Medical Group, Inc.

CHEMICAL DEPENDENCY RECOVERY PROGRAM
969 BROADWAY
OAKLAND, CALIFORNIA 94607
(510) 251-0121

PAUL T. MCDONALD, M.D. Physician-in-Chief	PRESTON MARING, M.D. Associate Physician-in-Chief	JOHN LOFTUS, M.D. Associate Physician-in-Chief
RICHARD BROWN, M.D. Assistant Physician-in-Chief	ANANSE TAHARKA, M.D. Assistant Physician-in-Chief	SHEILA MACKEL, M.D. Assistant Physician-in-Chief

J. DAVID ARTERBURN
Medical Group Administrator

Antioch
Davis
Fairfield
Fremont
Fresno
Gilroy
Hayward
Martinez
Milpitas
Mountain View
Napa
Novato
Oakland
Park Shadelands
Petaluma
Pleasanton
Rancho Cordova
Redwood City
Richmond
Roseville
Sacramento
San Francisco
San Jose
San Rafael
Santa Clara
Santa Rosa
S. Sacramento
S. San Francisco
Stockton
Vallejo
Walnut Creek

April 25, 2000

To Whom It May Concern:

I am writing this letter in support of LifeRing Secular Recovery. Kaiser Oakland's Chemical Dependency Recovery Program has been at 969 Broadway, Oakland since May of 1995. Ours is a regional program, drawing participants from Alameda and Contra Costa Counties and occasionally from Solano, and San Joaquin Counties. The Oakland CDRP offers four levels of care for chemically dependent people. Our population is a mix of voluntary and mandated patients. Some of our patients are struggling with addictive disease only, while others are dually diagnosed.

All the CDRP patients are required to go to outside support meetings. We offer traditional meetings such as NA and AA. We also offer LifeRing for patients who are not comfortable with the format of 12-step programs. LifeRing meetings have been offered on Tuesday and Wednesday since our program began. Last April LifeRing began a Saturday morning group. LifeRing meetings have always been well attended but the Saturday group has been so popular that at times we have had to open a second meeting room to accommodate all the people who wish to attend.

I am happy to state that LifeRing has always been able to coexist harmoniously with other support meetings. Patients report being satisfied with the format and some say they attend LifeRing and 12-step support meetings. I am happy to recommend LifeRing to any drug treatment program.

Sincerely Yours,

Jeffrey Blair MS MFCC
Day Treatment Co-coordinator

KAISER PERMANENTE

Letter of Recommendation, Kaiser Permanente CDRP, Oakland CA

On Saturday mornings at this large regional treatment facility, patients must attend their choice of one of the support groups that meet on the premises side by side: AA, NA and LifeRing. The groups co-exist harmoniously, and patients are satisfied. (Text of letter on next page)

(Text of letter on previous page)

April 25, 2000
To Whom It May Concern:

I am writing this letter in support of LifeRing Secular Recovery. Kaiser Oakland's Chemical Dependency Recovery Program has been at 969 Broadway, Oakland since May of 1995. Ours is a regional program, drawing participants from Alameda and Contra Costa Counties and occasionally from Solano, and San Joaquin Counties. The Oakland CDRP offers four levels of care for chemically dependent people. Our population is a mix of voluntary and mandated patients. Some of our patients are struggling with addictive disease only, while others are dually diagnosed.

All the CDRP patients are required to go to outside support meetings. We offer traditional meetings such as NA and AA. We also offer LifeRing for patients who are not comfortable with the format of 12-step programs. LifeRing meetings have been offered on Tuesday and Wednesday since our program began. Last April LifeRing began a Saturday morning group. LifeRing meetings have always been well attended but the Saturday group has been so popular that at times we have had to open a second meeting room to accommodate all the people who wish to attend.

I am happy to state that LifeRing has always been able to coexist harmoniously with other support meetings. Patients report being satisfied with the format and some say they attend LifeRing and 12-step support meetings. I am happy to recommend LifeRing to any drug treatment program.

Sincerely yours,

(signed)

Jeffrey Blair MS MFCC
Day Treatment Co-Coordinator

The Permanente Medical Group, Inc.
1201 FILLMORE STREET
SAN FRANCISCO, CALIFORNIA 94115-4110

April 26, 2000

Dear Marty, Gillian and Chardi,

Thanks again for coming to inform us about LifeRing Secular Recovery, it's history, principles and meetings. Your discussion opened a huge window for many staff, who will now be more active in referring patients to your groups to check them out.

As a matter of fact, one staff member asked me to see to it that the LifeRing schedule of meetings is put in every new patient's packet, along with 12 Step schedules. Progress, not perfection!

Sincerely,
Jerry

Letter of Acknowledgement, Kaiser Permanente CDRP, San Francisco

The LifeRing S.R. Service Center in Oakland, CA, may be able to send speakers to present the LifeRing approach to groups of staff and/or clients. (Text on next page)

(Text of letter on previous page)

Dear Marty, Gillian and Chandi,

Thanks again for coming to inform us about LifeRing Secular Recovery, its history, principles and meetings. Your discussion opened a huge window for many staff, who will now be more active in referring patients to your groups to check them out.

As a matter of fact, one staff member asked me to see to it that the LifeRing schedule of meetings is put in every new patient's packet, along with 12 Step Schedules.

Progress, not perfection!

Sincerely,

Wendy

Alta Bates

A SUTTER HEALTH AFFILIATE

April 5, 2000

To Whom It May Concern:

We are writing this letter to describe the invaluable work that Mr. Martin Nicolaus has done at Alta Bates Medical Center on 4 North Herrick, the Dual Diagnosis Unit. As a dual diagnosis crisis intervention facility, our patient population consists largely of persons who are suffering from psychiatric and mental health problems combined with a variety of substance abuse disorders. The majority of our patients arrive here against their will, having been placed on an involuntary psychiatric hold for observation and treatment because their psychiatric condition has caused them to be dangerous to themselves, or others, or gravely disabled and unable to care for themselves.

Since late 1998, Mr. Nicolaus has volunteered to lead a one hour weekly meeting of Life Ring Secular Recovery (formerly SOS) with our patients. Mr. Nicolaus brings to this group his personal life experience as an alcoholic in recovery. Much like the members of Alcoholics Anonymous and Narcotics Anonymous, he shares his own story of recovery, modeling a message of strength, hope and recovery for our despairing patients. As a volunteer, and a non-professional, Mr. Nicolaus also brings a model of self-help through community support to our patients.

The LifeRing group approach encourages patients to look within themselves and to each other for the strength to achieve abstinence and a healthier life style. Unlike the more traditional Alcoholics Anonymous approach, Life Ring does not use the concept "Higher Power" or the "12 Steps of Alcoholic's Anonymous." The philosophy and methods of LifeRing were developed as an alternative to AA for those people who need tools for recovery but have personal difficulty embracing the concept of "Higher Power." We have found that this approach encourages patients to begin to think positively about themselves and to find a reason to live productively. This approach resonates with the significant portion of our patients on 4 North who have received little or no benefit from past 12-Step involvement.

Although the Life Ring group's philosophy is different from the 12-Step model, we have not experienced any friction or strife as a result of adding the LifeRing meeting. We also offer AA to our patients . Our treatment team believes that there are many viable paths to recovery, LifeRing being one very positive adjunct to our traditional offerings. The LifeRing meeting is a bright spot in the patients' week ,and staff find that participation in the meeting enhances patients' motivation to get well.

Based on our experiences at this facility over the past two years, on behalf of the treatment team on 4 North, we would recommend similar LifeRing meetings to other facilities interested in expanding the range of their patient services.

Sincerely Yours,

Jane Haggstrom, R.N., Ph.D.
Patient Care Manager
4 North Herrick
Telephone: 510-204-4339

Alta Bates Medical Center
Herrick Campus, 2001 Dwight Way, Berkeley, CA 94704
Tel 510.204.4444

Letter of Recommendation, Alta Bates Hospital, Berkeley CA

LifeRing Secular Recovery volunteers may be available to lead self-help meetings in hospitals and institutions, such as this locked dual-diagnosis acute crisis intervention ward. (Text on next page)

(Text of letter on previous page)

April 5, 2000

To Whom It May Concern:

We are writing this letter to describe the invaluable work that Mr. Martin Nicolaus has done at Alta Bates Medical Center on 4 North Herrick, the Dual Diagnosis Unit. As a dual diagnosis crisis intervention facility, our patient population consists largely of persons who are suffering from psychiatric and mental health problems combined with a variety of substance abuse disorders. The majority of our patients arrive here against their will, having been placed on an involuntary psychiatric hold for observation and treatment because their psychiatric condition has caused them to be dangerous to themselves, to others, or gravely disabled and unable to care for themselves.

Since late 1998, Mr. Nicolaus has volunteered to lead a one hour weekly meeting of LifeRing Secular Recovery (formerly SOS) with our patients. Mr. Nicolaus brings to this group his personal life experience as an alcoholic in recovery. Much like the members of Alcoholics Anonymous and Narcotics Anonymous, he shares his own story of recovery, modeling a message of strength, hope and recovery for our despairing patients. As a volunteer, and a non-professional, Mr. Nicolaus also brings a model of self-help through community support to our patients.

The LifeRing group approach encourages patients to look within themselves and to each other for the strength to achieve abstinence and a healthier life style. Unlike the more traditional Alcoholics Anonymous approach, Life Ring does not use the concept "Higher Power" or the "12 Steps of Alcoholic's Anonymous." The philosophy and methods of LifeRing were developed as an alternative to AA for those people who need tools for recovery but have personal difficulty embracing the concept of "Higher Power." We have found that this approach encourages patients to begin to think positively about themselves and to find a reason to live productively. This approach resonates with the significant portion of our patients on 4 North who have received little or no benefit from past 12-Step involvement.

Although the Life Ring group's philosophy is different from the 12-Step model, we have not experienced any friction or strife as a result of adding the LifeRing meeting. We also offer AA to our patients. Our treatment team believes that there are many viable paths to recovery, LifeRing being one very positive adjunct to our traditional offerings. The LifeRing meeting is a bright spot in the patients' week, and staff find that participation in the meeting enhances patients' motivation to get well.

Based on our experiences at this facility over the past two years, on behalf of the treatment team on 4 North, we would recommend similar LifeRing meetings to other facilities interested in expanding the range of their patient services.

Sincerely Yours,

(signed)

Jane Haggstrom, R.N., Ph.D.
Patient Care Manager
4 North Herrick
Telephone 510-204-4339

[Notes]

Frequently Asked Questions About LifeRing Secular Recovery

Is LifeRing an abstinence-based organization?

LifeRing Secular Recovery is an abstinence organization. We teach the "Sobriety Priority" and our motto is "Don't Drink Or Use, No Matter What." We define abstinence as zero consumption of alcohol and "drugs." Individuals who want to experiment with moderation, or who define abstinence as something other than zero consumption, would not find their desires supported in LifeRing.

Is LifeRing only for alcoholics?

LifeRing Secular Recovery welcomes individuals with any substance addiction problem, be it alcohol, street drugs, or abuse of prescription drugs. We do not segregate alcoholics from other addicts. We view all substance addictions as basically the same and we understand that poly-addiction is typical, rather than exceptional. Therefore we are a poly-abstinence organization. While we do not require LifeRing participants to quit using tobacco products, we encourage and support our members to do so as soon as they feel ready.

How does LifeRing deal with people who have strong religious beliefs?

LifeRing welcomes people with any kind of religious beliefs, or with no religious beliefs at all. We are strictly secular. We never ask members what their religious or spiritual beliefs are. Participants can keep whatever religious beliefs or disbeliefs they have. Our meetings avoid practices such as prayer that would raise religious issues. We close, instead, with a round of applause and encouragement to one another for staying sober. Participants who want religious or spiritual guidance are encouraged to turn to the established churches, temples and other providers.

If you don't use a Higher Power, how can people get sober?

Inside each person who comes to us with an addiction problem there are two forces at work: the addicted part, that wants the person to drink and use and die, and the healthy part, that wants the person to quit and be clean and sober and live. In our LifeRing groups we mutually reinforce the healthy parts within ourselves and each other, until our sober side achieves a resilient dominance over our addicted side. Our method does not require a Higher Power. It's based on social interaction. Further reading: *How Our Self-Help Support Groups Work*, in this volume at Page 23.

Since you don't have Steps, what therapeutic techniques do you use?

Our basic therapeutic technique is group support for individual effort. We support each individual's motivation to get sober and we try to offer people a wide range of tools with which to construct their own personal recovery program. It has been called a "cafeteria" approach, and a "do it yourself" approach. We do not require or "suggest" any particular therapeutic protocol; our motto is "whatever works for you." In very general terms our method stems from cognitive behaviorist and motivational-enhancement perspectives, but we are not disciples of any particular philosopher and we do not act as a delivery vehicle for any particular method or technology. We are an umbrella for all kinds of secular, abstinence-based therapeutic approaches. We have an open-ended workbook for those who want to build their individual programs in writing. "Informed eclecticism" is a good description of our outlook. "Individualized recovery" is another apt label. "Strength-based" is an accurate term for our approach. Further reading: *Where Does the LifeRing Recovery Approach Fit Within the Spectrum of Contemporary Treatment Methods* at Page 49 and *A Clinical Protocol Based on the Sober Self-Empowerment Concept at Page 63* in this volume; also: *Handbook of Secular Recovery*, see Further Readings at Page 77 this volume.

What happens at your meetings? What do people do?

LifeRing meetings exist so that people can give each other support to live clean and sober lives. For this reason our meetings tend to be focused on the "here and now" – on current events in the participants' lives. Formats vary with the meeting. Some meetings use a topic system, some don't. But all of our meetings allow cross-talk. In an ideal meeting, the atmosphere is comfortable and informal, like a conversational gathering in a living room. If a meeting gets larger than 15-20 people, we will try to split it into two meetings so that everyone gets a chance to participate. Further reading: *Handbook of Secular Recovery*, see Page 77.

Are LifeRing meetings led by treatment professionals?

LifeRing meetings are led by ordinary members. Generally, the members with more sober time take turns at meeting leadership. We suggest a six-month rotation. We do hold workshops for meeting leaders, but these are not a requirement. Treatment professionals have helped new meetings get off the ground, but their primary objective in so doing is to turn over leadership to lay participants as soon as practicable. Further reading: *Handbook of Secular Recovery*, see Page 77.

Do you have sponsors?

The LifeRing concept is extremely simple. The newcomer can grasp it completely from Day One. Therefore we have no need for expert guides to lead the beginner through it. The LifeRing approach emphasizes personal initiative and personal responsibility. We are hesitant about relationships that involve members giving up control over their recovery to some other member, no matter how experienced. We value bonding among members, but on a voluntary, peer-to-peer basis. We do encourage people at meetings to exchange telephone numbers and contact each other outside meetings.

What about codependents?

People who are involved in relationships where drinking/using is a problem are welcome to attend our meetings, either alone or in company with their significant other. If there are enough codependents, they can form their own meeting, and they might meet at the same time as the drinkers/users but in another room.

What about people with dual diagnosis?

LifeRing is open to individuals who have a chemical dependency problem and who have also been diagnosed with depression, bipolar disorder or the like. We support dually diagnosed individuals in understanding that alcohol and street drugs are not appropriate medications for their other disorders. We may encourage such individuals to get additional professional help and explore additional support group options for their other diagnosis. Psychotropic medications prescribed by a physician with knowledge of the patient's history of substance addiction do not violate the Sobriety Priority and we urge participants to take such medications strictly in accordance with their physician's prescription.

Does LifeRing subscribe to the Disease Theory?

LifeRing does not take an official position on the etiology of substance addiction. We understand that the classification of alcoholism as a medical disease is key to public and private funding of treatment. Most of our leading members tend to view addiction as primarily a physiological disorder caused by excessive drinking/using. Hereditary predisposition may, but need not, play a role. Most of us tend to discount psychoanalytical, moral and/or spiritual theories of addiction. However, LifeRing members are free to hold whatever beliefs on this issue they feel useful to their recovery, and we sometimes have lively, informative internal debates on the issue. Our experience has been that people who do and people who don't subscribe to the disease theory can both stay sober.

Does LifeRing believe in members doing service?

We are a service organization. We exist so that alcoholics and addicts can have the LifeRing option available for their recovery. We save lives. However, whether individuals just come to meetings, put a dollar in the basket, and leave, or whether they want to do more -- that's up to them. Some of our members lead meetings in hospitals, treatment centers, and prisons (see Pages 7-11 above). Others don't. We don't pressure them. However, we wouldn't exist as an organization without individuals who donate their time and energy and other resources to make LifeRing Recovery available to others. Such people are the core of our membership. We call them "convenors" – people who bring people together.

Are there any scientific studies proving the efficacy of the LifeRing approach?

There are as many scientific studies – that is, double-blind longitudinal studies with control groups – proving the efficacy of the LifeRing approach as there are such studies proving the efficacy of the 12-Step approach. LifeRing invites qualified social scientists who want to conduct such a study to contact the LSR Service Center at the address given on the copyright page of this volume. (For further reading on this topic, see *Where Does the LifeRing Approach Fit Within the Spectrum of Contemporary Treatment Methods* at Page 49 in this volume.)

How does LifeRing compare to other alternative recovery organizations?

LifeRing S.R. is part of a broader cultural trend toward secularism in recovery that began in the 1970s. The first organization of this type was Women for Sobriety, founded by Jean Kirkpatrick in 1975. WFS advocates a positive, self-affirming recovery concept. The LifeRing approach has a great deal in common with that inspiration. The next group to emerge was Secular Sobriety Groups (SSG) founded by James Christopher in 1985; this changed to Secular Organizations for Sobriety (SOS) in 1988, and became a subsidiary of the

Council for Secular Humanism. LifeRing S.R. arose out of SOS; it continues the original secular sobriety philosophy of SSG/SOS but is self-governing and independent of outside affiliation. Rational Recovery (RR) arose at about the same time as SSG. Founded by Jack Trimpey, it currently markets a proprietary recovery technology known as Addictive Voice Recognition Training (AVRT®). RR has dissolved its self-help support groups and withdrawn from the recovery movement. An outgrowth of RR is SMART (Self-Management And Recovery Training), which organizes groups based on the Rational Emotive Behavior Therapy (REBT) technique developed by philosopher Albert Ellis. The leadership of SMART has included prominent advocates of moderation. Many LifeRing members view REBT and AVRT® as potentially useful tools among others, but LifeRing does not support moderationist aims. In all of its relations with other groups, 12-Step or other, LifeRing tries to stress our commonality of interests, avoid unnecessary friction, and work cooperatively.

How is LifeRing organized?

All individuals in leading positions in LifeRing S.R. are themselves in recovery from a substance addiction. Most are lay people, not recovery professionals. At this time unpaid volunteers fill all positions. LifeRing is low-budget but financially independent, supported by passing the basket at meetings and by individual donations. We are chartered as a nonprofit, and donations are tax-deductible. The internal organizational process of LifeRing Secular Recovery is still under construction, but will be democratic and meeting-centered.

Does LifeRing have its own clinics or treatment centers?

LifeRing is a network of peer-led self-help support groups. We hold meetings in a number of treatment centers and institutions, but so far we have not attempted to develop our approach as a clinical protocol in its own right. One interesting movement in this direction has been developed independently at the Kaiser Permanente CDRP facilities in Hawaii; see *A Clinical Protocol Based on the Sober Self-Empowerment Concept* at Page 63 in this volume. We are in the process of publishing a workbook designed for solo and group use, entitled "My Personal Recovery Plan." (See back cover.)

If we allow LifeRing groups at our treatment centers, will this undermine our 12-Step program or cause friction?

LifeRing groups have been active at traditional treatment centers for well over five years without any significant friction. See, Letters of Reference, in this volume, p. 7. LifeRing is an abstinence-based program, and its presence reinforces the basic message of the facility's protocol. LifeRing groups offer an environment where individuals who are uncomfortable with the 12-Step approach can work on their recoveries in their own way, relieving patient/staff tensions within the treatment environment. LifeRing does not interfere with, but operates as a supplement to, a facility's treatment regimen. Where patients are presented with a choice, they develop a deeper commitment to the path they eventually select. In this way, the presence of a secular option like LifeRing is beneficial to all concerned.

[Notes]

How (Our) Self-Help Support Groups Work

By Marty N.

Excerpted from www.unhooked.com, the home page of LifeRing Secular Recovery

When I have the privilege to address treatment professionals about the LifeRing recovery approach, one of the most frequent questions is "how it works." By way of introduction, I would like to quote a passage from an article by Prof. Edward C. Senay, Emeritus Professor of Psychiatry and Director of Research, Interventions, University of Chicago. In his contribution to the college text *Substance Abuse, A Comprehensive Textbook, 3d Ed*, 1997, edited by Lowinson et al., Dr. Senay writes:

> The majority of substance abusers [...] are intensely ambivalent, which means that there is another psychological pole, separate from and opposite to denial, that is in delicate, frequently changing balance with denial and that is a pole of healthy striving. Most substance abusers are quite aware that what they are doing is destructive, that they have been deceived by the culture of drugs and alcohol, and that they want to change. If this were not true, there would be no Alcoholics Anonymous, Cocaine Anonymous, or Narcotics Anonymous [...]. The job of a clinician is to appeal to this pole of healthy striving. Even for those in complete denial, one must assume that there is a positive pole, because one can be sure that it was not there only in retrospect. ("*Diagnostic Interview and Mental Status Examination*," in Lowinson, *op. cit.*, p. 364).

Whenever I am asked to explain theoretically what we do in LifeRing meetings and "how it works," I begin by drawing the outline of a head on the board, and within it I sketch a large area labeled "A" that represents the addiction, and a smaller area labeled "S" that represents its opposite - what Prof. Senay calls the "pole of healthy striving." (Figure 1, next page).

This sketch -- meant purely as a metaphor, not as a picture of brain anatomy -- represents the alcoholic or addict as they usually stand at the beginning of recovery. That is to say, the

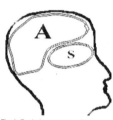

"A" or addicted element within them is large and dominant, the "S" or sober element is comparatively smaller, and the "A" overshadows it. The actual relation between these poles in a real person is, as Prof. Senay aptly points out, an ever-changing balance; but the sketch approximates the average state of a typical person at the start of getting sober.

Fig. 1: Beginning recovery. The "addict" part of the brain overshadows the "sober" part.

We have many names for the "A" part of the picture. We call it the addiction, or the disease, or the lizard brain, or the Beast, or the Devil, and many others. But oddly, we have a paucity of names for the pole of healthy striving. In the groups I lead, I sometimes call it the sober place, or the sober self, or I personify it as the Sober Guy or the Sober Gal -- the Sober Me -- within. Whatever its name, by the time an alcoholic or addict shows up on the radar screen of a recovery program or a recovery self-help support group, it is usually active and visible to the discerning eye.

Two main kinds of evidence tell us that a sober place or sober "self" is present within the person. The first is the psychological experience of inner dialogue. I have spoken with hundreds of alcoholics and/or addicts in various stages of wetness and dryness, and almost without exception they report having conversations -- arguments -- in their heads about their drinking and using. Typically there is one set of voices arguing for getting wasted, but another set arguing against it. (Fig. 2, next page.) The active user's inner conflict over drinking and using, which may appear on the surface as "ambivalence," is one sure sign that the force of addiction within the person is not the only occupant, and that a lesser but opposite presence is also active within. Inner conflict over drinking/using is one of the almost universally shared experiences of our subculture.

The other class of evidence that tells us that there is some kind of element or force for sobriety within the alcoholic/addict in recovery is the existence of self-help recovery organizations. As everyone knows, the only requirement for membership in

Fig. 2: Inner dialogue. The desire to get clean and sober arises from the sober self.

them (and our own group is no different in this respect) "is a sincere desire to get sober." We know with certainty that a sincere desire to get sober does not originate from the diseased or addicted force within the person. It must arise from an opposite force, a force of health and of anti-addiction -- a sober place within. Without that "pole of healthy striving" within the addict, as Prof. Senay observed, no self-help groups could exist.

If we start to deconstruct the "sober place" within an active or recently active alcoholic/addict, we will probably find several sources. Part of it is the remnant of the person's pre-addicted life -- the years of childhood and perhaps of other periods in life when the person functioned without drinking/using. Part of it stems from the kind of primitive reflex-like survival instinct that makes even a depressed, suicidal person fight for air when someone pushes their head under water. Part of it is the emotional deposit left by waves of harmful consequences from our drinking/using. Part of it may stem, as the neuropharmacologist Elliot Gardner has suggested, from the binary chemistry of the drugs of addiction themselves: in the short term they trigger the pleasure circuits, but they also activate slower "opponent" chemicals that are anti-rewarding and make us want to stop. [Gardner, "*Brain Reward Mechanisms*" in Lowinson, op.cit. p. 68]. Part of it represents our persistent rational reflection that there has got to be a better way.

The sober pole within an addicted person is a complex construction of many layers and pieces. It would be useful to know more about how this element slumbering within the active drinker/user comes to assert itself and to influence behavior. We do know that if the pole of sober striving within the person remains dormant and subordinate to the addictive pole, then the addiction will sooner or later consume them and they will die of the consequences.

Experience shows that this fatal negative imbalance of power inside the addict can change and be reversed if two or more come together in an environment of support for sobriety. In what follows, I attempt to sketch how the self-help group process works to yield recoveries.

The group environment and its rules are clearly important. We know, for example, that if two individuals who are constituted as described in Fig. 1 meet in a bar or a drug house or some similar environment, for the purpose of drinking/using, then typically the communication will run between the addicted part of the two heads, and the interchange will reinforce the addiction. "Have a drink" - "Let's get wasted." This is addicted self talking to addicted self. (Fig. 3) This kind of interaction notoriously adds weight to the addiction in both heads at the expense of the sober strivings. This is the vicious cycle of addiction. Drinking and drugging environments are not only

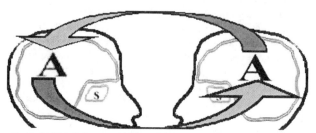

Fig. 3: Addict-Addict communication, as in a bar or drug house, expands the influence of the addicted portions and shrinks the sober portions.

fueling stations for the substance, they are support groups for the behavior. They are places where the person gets strokes for drinking/drugging and sympathy for enduring the consequences.

Sobriety support group environments -- sound ones, in any event -- are designed to shut down addict-addict bonding and to promote positive exchanges between the sober selves instead. This design is partly explicit, and partly implied. For example, the opening statements of most of our meetings expressly bar persons from speaking if they are under the influence. On the other hand, no written rule forbids sober meeting participants from discussing, for example, the merits of different kinds of wines or liquors, or the best growing regions for sinsemilla. But participants would recognize implicitly that this kind of topic celebrates drinking/drugging, and awakens and stimulates the addicted brain region. Someone who ventured into this area would be met with silence or a change of subject.

The written and unwritten prohibitions of a sobriety support group aim to isolate the addicted parts of the participating brains from one another, to deprive them of social stimulus, to deactivate them and as far as possible put them to sleep. What we are trying to awaken, to foster and to protect is communication from and to the sober places within one another, as in Fig. 4. Sober talking to sober is the channel where we want the traffic. The objective is to connect the sober places with each other, and to stimulate their activity and raise their energy level.

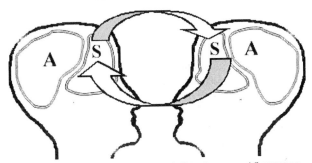

Fig. 4: Sober-sober communication expands the sober areas at the expense of the addicted parts.

What flows through this communications channel is at first sight "just words." (There is of course also nonverbal communication, facial expressions, body language.) However, words have the power to change feelings and thereby to change behavior. If I am feeling lonely and I come to you and say "I feel lonely," I will probably feel less lonely as soon as the words reach your ears. Similarly, if we feel angry, or frustrated, or any number of things, we can change those feelings by speaking them to others who hear us. This "magic" is the basis of all talk therapy. Even tangles of terrifying feelings that twist our bodily tissues in knots can be released through talk. [Judith Hermann, M.D., *Trauma and Recovery*, N.Y. 1997, p. 183].

Sober-sober communication is a win-win transaction; it creates pluses at both ends. "I am sober today." By voicing that statement to you, I affirm my sobriety and make it public to you. This is a plus for my sober self. With these simple factual words, heard by you, my sober self is celebrating an achievement. And you, who hear this statement, also experience a plus. If you were unsure that sobriety is possible, you may take encouragement. You may take it as a stimulus to do likewise. You may take it as comfort that you are not alone in your own sobriety. And if you respond, "I also am sober today," the effect is doubled. You again experience a plus; and so do I, hearing you. A bond is built between the sober parts within us, and the sobriety within both of us grows larger, stronger and deeper.

What holds for simple affirmations goes also for the more complex communications that take place in most self-help meetings. For example, a member shares an anecdote from the previous week: "I was at my brother's house and he offered me a beer. And I said, no thank you, I don't drink anymore, and I didn't." Often, a statement like this will bring applause from the group. Applause from the group is a powerful method of social reinforcement. This anecdote sends strong positive messages. The speaker made a decision to prioritize sobriety over sibling ties. He defined himself as a non-drinker. He stuck to his sober guns. Everyone who hears the anecdote mentally analyzes it from various angles and applies it to their own situation. It is stored away in memory for the occasion when it may be needed. It becomes part of everyone's sobriety tool kit. Over time, each participant hears and shares hundreds of such experiences and builds them into a mental mosaic that is a meaningful guide to action for that individual.

The desired result of such an accumulation of pluses over time is the resilient dominance of the sober self. The important thing is the resilience. During the hour that the person spends in a well-functioning sobriety meeting, the sober place within the mind is dominant. The sober self is active and has the run of the brain. It hums with the energy derived from the immediate connection with the other sober selves. This is the beneficial cycle of sobriety. The addicted portion, during that hour, is isolated, disconnected, and inactive. The problem is to maintain this temporary sober dominance and make it enduring. When the meeting is over and the sober minds unplug from one another, the sober striving tends to retreat and the inner addiction to revive. This is why no single meeting is enough. It may take a great deal of time, many repetitions, and the accumulation of a great many "pluses" before the dominance of the sober force within the brain becomes tenacious, so that over time and on the average, the person's makeup comes to resemble Fig. 5, in which the sober part overshadows the addiction.

By the evidence, the addicted portion never disappears completely. People may experience catastrophic relapses after ten, fifteen, twenty years or even longer. Nor is the

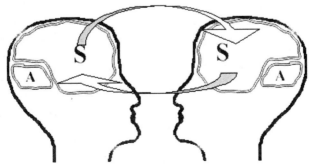

Fig. 5: Successful recovery: sober area has resilient dominance over addicted part

addicted portion "dead." It can continue to generate mentation and emotional activity for life. Accordingly, the new positive imbalance in the mind is not a static end result, a final fate, any more than its opposite, the dominance of the addicted self, was a final fate. The inner dialogues do not disappear, but this time they have a different outcome, and because of that they are experienced not as tortures, but as affirmations, even as celebrations. The person started recovery as an addict who has a sober self locked up within; the person becomes transformed during the recovery process into a sober person who has an addicted self locked within. That is the only difference, but it is a profound one.

Although the images I have sketched are not intended as pictures of brain anatomy, the basic process is consistent with psychobiologist D.O. Hebb's rule that "the strength of a synapse between two neurons is increased by the repeated activation of one neuron by the other across this synapse." (Hebb, 1949). Both the strengthening of the sober circuitry and the corresponding atrophy and reduction of the addicted brain networks through repeated social activation and non-use, respectively, exemplify basic patterns of brain development. (Siegel, *The Developing Mind, Toward a Neurobiology of Interpersonal Experience* (Guilford Press, NY 1999), pp. 13-14).

I believe that the foregoing process describes -- in a very generalized, schematic way, to be sure -- how our self-help recovery groups work. I base this description on having attended something approaching a thousand of our meetings over the past seven years and more. Although I have attended only a few meetings of other kinds of self-help groups, and have never participated in an AA or NA meeting, I will be so bold as to conjecture that when they work at all, they all work approximately this way. Prof. Senay's observations quoted at the outset suggest that this dynamic between the two contending "poles" within the person is what makes possible the existence of self-help groups in general.

On several occasions when I have presented these thoughts and diagrams before audiences of people familiar with the 12-

Step process, I have been told that "this is exactly what we do also." And indeed, there is much in the AA universe that resonates with this description of the healing process. There is the image of AA as "two drunks talking;" there is the emphasis on the sharing of "experience, strength and hope," and much else. Yet, as soon as my interlocutors tell me that what I have described is exactly what they also do, they feel assailed by doubts. The process of mutual self-help I have described relies on communication among humans. The healing power comes from a specific purposeful kind of interaction between people, much as fire comes from skillfully and persistently rubbing two sticks together. Reflecting on this, my interlocutors grow confused. This sounds so right, so intuitively correct, so much in accord with experience -- but what about the "Higher Power"? The therapeutic process here described has no need of a "Higher Power" hypothesis.

Reduced to its barest essentials, the road map that we sketch for the newly recovering person comes down to these few words: *empower your sober self.* In Prof. Senay's words, "the job of the clinician is to appeal to this pole of healthy striving." For us, as LifeRing participants, the job is to help one another find and recognize this "Sober Me" within us, and to assist one another in reinforcing that place, extending its influence over our behavior, and increasing its energy level, until it becomes the dominant force within us, overshadowing the addicted side. This is what it means to make sobriety one's priority. This process is not easy or quick. However, the concept is so clear and simple that a newcomer can grasp it on day one, and it supplies enough challenges to last a lifetime.

For more information about the LifeRing S.R. meeting process, see *Handbook of Secular Recovery*, in Further Readings on page 77.

[Notes]

Historical Roots and Antecedents of the LifeRing Approach

(Review of *Slaying the Dragon: The History of Addiction Treatment and Recovery in America,* by *William L. White (1998)* Chestnut Health Systems / Lighthouse Institute, ISBN 0-938475-07-X).

William White's book is a history of the alcoholism treatment and recovery effort in the U.S., written for treatment professionals and laypersons. It has a wonderful cover photo showing nearly a hundred gentlemen of the 19th century posed under a sign that says "THE LAW MUST RECOGNIZE A LEADING FACT, MEDICAL NOT PENAL TREATMENT REFORMS THE DRUNKARD." It is one of those delightful history books that are heavy on detail and light on argument, so that even if you don't share the author's bias you can find lots of nuggets.

It is commendable also in that the author has a broader social eye than the average, and includes Native Americans, Blacks, women and other historically neglected people in his chronicle

George Copway (Kah-ge-ga-gah-bowh), Ojibway Temperance Reformer

from the outset. Indeed, he is quotable; he says about the African slaves, for example, that there is little evidence of a liquor problem among them, and "the major alcohol problem for early African Americans was the risk they faced when Whites drank it." And did you know that the very earliest recorded mutual self-help societies of alcoholics were created by Native Americans? "Our first evidence of individuals turning their own negative experiences with alcohol into a social movement of mutual support occurs within Native American tribes." That was as early as 1772, and perhaps goes to explain why a successful mutual support group today can evoke the feeling of belonging to a special kind of close-knit tribe.

A good history makes us humble by showing us how little there is in our strivings that is genuinely new. White's is a good history. The concept of alcoholism as a disease, which some people claim is as modern as Saran Wrap, was already articulated by Benjamin Rush, the Surgeon General of George Washington's revolutionary armies, in a pamphlet dated 1784. Rush was also one of the first to prescribe total abstinence from spirits as the sole remedy: "taste not, handle not, touch not." He saw treatment of drunkenness as a political issue: "A nation corrupted by alcohol can never be free." He had a very modern multi-factorial view of alcoholism's causes and he articulated a multiple-pathway model of recovery. Although some of his measures were archaic by current standards -- massive doses of medicine and copious bleeding -- he was a hugely insightful and modern figure.

Older than the disease theory itself is the opposition to it. When Rush advanced his theses, he was conscious of getting "a cold reception." Drinking in colonial America was an everyday habit, and penurious inebriates were flogged or jailed, never hospitalized. The consensus of religious leaders was that moderate drinking was a gift of God, but drunkenness was a vice and a sin. Fast forward a century. A group of 14 physicians and their supporters met in New York in November 1870 to found the American Association for the Cure of Inebriates, and published a manifesto whose opening sentence was "Intemperance is a disease." Vehement debate within the ranks followed, and months later the directors of the Franklin Reformatory Home for Inebriates in Philadelphia resigned from the association, stating "We do not, either in our name or management, recognize drunkenness as the effect of a diseased impulse; but regard it as a habit, sin and crime; we do not speak of cases being cured, as in a hospital, but 'reformed.'" [p. 26]. The wonderful cover photograph with its slogan, so evocative of our current debate over the "War on Drugs," dates from the early 1890s.

Equally old is the debate between the religious and the secular paths of recovery. The very first mutual self-help movement among European Americans was the Washingtonians. Six artisans and workingmen started the "Washingtonian Total

Abstinence Society" in a Baltimore tavern on April 2, 1840. The movement took off like a rocket. It celebrated its first anniversary with a parade of 5,000 people. Two years later, a public meeting of the Society in Boston drew 12,000 people. At its peak, it reached many hundreds of thousands, including an active women's division ("Total abstinence or no husband!" went one slogan) and a weekly newspaper. Abraham Lincoln addressed one of its meetings. The Washingtonians operated as "secular missionaries." They went to taverns to recruit. They divided the cities into wards and had committees assigned to recruit the drunks in each area to come to meetings and take the pledge. Washingtonians, or most of them, "believed that social camaraderie was sufficient to sustain sobriety and that a religious component would only discourage drinkers from joining." [13]. Clergy were excluded from the meetings, and some accused the Washingtonians of "the heresy of humanism -- elevating their own will above God's by failing to include religion in their meetings." This was in 1842!

The Washingtonians were hugely important in shaping future self-help movements. It was they who introduced among white men the practice at meetings of sharing experiences, in lieu of making abstract speeches. It was they who first held closed, alcoholics-only meetings. It was they who first enlisted the reformed drunkard as missionary to the drinker, pioneering the concept of service as a tool of self-recovery. They sustained members' sobriety through regular weekly fellowship meetings, encouraged all manner of sober recreation, involved women and other family members in their process, and founded some of the first "homes" where drunkards could go to dry out and live in sober communities.

The Washingtonians were also totally disorganized. They had no central authority

Washingtonian Home in Chicago (1850s)

through which the movement's philosophy or program could be defined and sustained against diversion. For example, two leading speakers on the national stage who portrayed themselves as spokesmen of this vastly popular cause held pro-religious views at variance with the consensus of the movement's membership, and used the movement's fame to line their own pockets with lecture fees -- and the Society had no effective means to prevent it. Because of their "organizational ineptitude," their message became confused; they could not articulate a sustained road forward, they failed to raise up sustainable leadership, and their energy and numbers dissipated almost as quickly as they had risen. But their substantive legacy is alive today in every LifeRing Secular Recovery meeting, and in every other alcoholics' and addicts' self-help meeting as well.

After the disintegration of the Washingtonians came the fraternal temperance societies and reform clubs. Their day was the middle decades of the 1800s. The fraternal societies provided the reformed drunkard with a sober support system. They were secret. They were organized hierarchically and they offered stability. These early sobrietists' fraternities, such as the Sons of Temperance, the Good Templars, the Good Samaritans and others were secular. They did not rely on religious conversion as the sole means of personal reform, but focused more on mutual social support and surveillance as means of achieving and maintaining sobriety. The Good Samaritans broke new ground by admitting all races.

As the fraternal societies dwindled, the Reform Clubs rose. These were largely businessmen's abstinence clubs -- although a few had moderation as their goal -- and their fortunes rose and fell with their individual leaders. Most of these were gone by the dawn of the 20th century. It seems fair to say, in retrospect, that virtually every trend and tendency we see in the alcohol-recovery universe around us today was already present a century ago.

White really warms to his subject in Section II of the book, which deals with early treatment institutions and approaches. We learn here about the 19th century medical researchers -- it was a Swedish physician, Magnus Huss, who first applied the term alcoholism to the syndrome -- and about the first asylums, homes, farms, colonies and other institutions for dipsomaniacs. The bad blood that sometimes exists today between the addiction field and psychiatry is traced back to an early institutional conflict. Heads of the insane asylums did not want to have inebriates there, because it would damage the reputation of their facilities. Heads of inebriate treatment facilities equally did not want to send inebriates to the early insane asylums, where free and liberal use of whiskey, opium and other drugs, both among patients and staff, were more the rule than the exception.

There was a vast array of conflicting opinions in the addiction treatment field, each one propounded with an air of total authority. White deserves credit for seeing the patient's viewpoint amidst this dogmatic cacophony. He quotes one opiate addict in the 1880s:

"I have borne the most unfair comments and insinuations from people utterly incapable of comprehending for one second the smallest part of my suffering, or even knowing that such could exist. Yet they claim to deliver opinions and comments as though better informed on the subject ... than anybody else in the world. I have been stung by their talk as by hornets, and have been driven to solitude to avoid the fools."

There is a lovely chapter examining these institutions from the inside. Many patients stayed on as paid workers there, and the debate over the relative merits of former addicts v. non-addict professionals was already a live one then. Among the patients at the typical center, physicians, lawyers, engineers, druggists, journalists, artists, students, reporters, clergymen and actors were the most frequently represented occupations, in that order. Etiology was hotly debated. One prominent theorist defined "drunkenness" as a moral vice of the lower classes requiring punishment, whereas "inebriety" was a disease of the higher classes, meriting rest and renewal. There was a full panoply of treatment methods, many of them not very different from today's. Outcomes varied greatly and information was sparse, with claimed but not widely credited

5-year abstinence rates of one third to two thirds. And around this time inebriety among women first penetrated public notice, and a halting start was made at comprehension and treatment. The author adds four chapters that examine individual treatment centers of this era in particular detail.

By 1925 most of these treatment centers had collapsed. They represented the first cohesive institutional attempt to treat addiction as a medical problem. They pioneered physiological explanations of inebriety and physical methods of treatment. They shifted the dialogue from moral and religious failings to medical vulnerability. Yet they failed to articulate any cohesive and demonstrably effective treatment philosophy that could seduce public opinion away from the conviction that the way to deal with drunkards was to outlaw alcohol and to throw offenders in jail. The enactment of Prohibition was the death knell of these pioneer addiction treatment institutes.

There is an interesting chapter on the Keeley Institutes, a hugely successful chain of privately owned miracle cure centers purveying injections of a secret formula allegedly based on chlorides of gold, which supposedly took away all desire to drink or use drugs or tobacco. The formula was later shown to be placebo. The Keeley Institutes helped many thousands of alcoholics to achieve long-term abstinence in the 1890s and later. The secret formula, says the author, was "a gimmick that engaged addicts' propensity for magical thinking and helped them through the early weeks and months of recovery." The real curative power lay in the spirit of mutual

Keeley League No. 1 in open-air session, Dwight, Illinois. (Cover)

support and self-respect engendered by the Institutes'
treatment and post-treatment protocols.

In this era, there was also a plethora of other alleged magic
cures for inebriety, unaccompanied by the costlier treatment
and support regimen available to the more affluent. Most of
the miracle potions contained, not surprisingly, alcohol,
cocaine and opiates. They were gradually driven back by
legislation.

Religious conversion as a treatment method earns a special
chapter in the book. Religious leaders had been preaching
since time immemorial that what the alcoholic needed was to
find God, and alcoholics have been testifying to salvation
through faith as long as there have been revival meetings. As
America's urban problems worsened toward the end of the
century, a few religious converts determined to bring God to
the alcoholic. This chapter details the work of Jerry McAuley,
an ex-convict and ex-Catholic who became a born-again
evangelical Protestant and launched numerous Skid Row
rescue missions. He became a beloved figure because he
reached out to the homeless and destitute alcoholics whom the
established churches considered as undeserving of God's
grace. Evangelical Protestantism also created the Salvation
Army, which has worked since the 1890s to bring deliverance
to the alcoholic "through submission of the total personality to
the Lordship of Jesus Christ." William James' 1902 essay,
"The Varieties of Religious Experience," was an influential
philosophical statement of the religious conversion theory of
alcoholism treatment. James described in detail the
accoutrements of a conversion experience (voices, visions,
lights, awareness of superior power, raptures, etc.) and
concluded, in a famous epigram, "the only cure for
dipsomania is religiomania." The chapter concludes with a
too-brief review of early criticisms of the religious conversion
theory. Religious leaders of less charismatic or evangelical
leanings pointed out that conversion experiences occur to only
a small number of believers. Others worried that religious
conversion would be turned into merely a tool to achieve
sobriety, rather than an end in itself. A Connecticut state
report expressed concern that religious conversion could be

more harmful than beneficial inasmuch as it frequently had the unhealthy side effect of promoting religious fanaticism.

Two chapters of this encyclopedic work discuss, respectively, the physical and the psychological treatment approaches to alcoholism found in the American arsenal prior to World War II. Here is discussion of sterilization, various nutritional regimes, exercise, leisure, work, sun baths, a great variety of water cures, early drug therapies (frequently involving morphine!), electrical and chemical convulsion therapy, lobotomy, and miscellaneous others, including infecting alcoholics with gonorrhea because this allegedly reduced their craving to drink. The eye then turns toward the psychological approaches. There is a remarkably balanced discussion of psychoanalysis (judged worthless as therapy but indirectly helpful as a philosophy because it helped to legitimize therapy by lay persons), and the work of prominent psychologically informed medical specialists of the 1930s. There is an extended discussion of aversion therapy as practiced by Shadel and his followers; this had good reported outcomes and was the most enduring behavioral technique in the first six decades of this century. The focus then turns to other drug addictions, chronicling the influence of Freud in legitimizing cocaine as a "cure" for opiate addiction, and detailing the medical profession's loss of control over these drugs as the federal government intervened to criminalize their use.

The author then turns to Alcoholics Anonymous, whose history and impact occupy the following four chapters. When White's historical panorama reaches the 1930s, the period of the founding of Alcoholics Anonymous, there is a marked softening in the focus. It is always most difficult to write about the things one is closest to, and there is much evidence in the book that the author is very close to AA indeed.

Nevertheless, this is not merely history as "lives of the saints." Indeed, there is much in the work that will make the shuttered dodecamaniac intensely uncomfortable.

White cites evidence, for example, that at the time of the famous conversion experience in which AA founder Bill W. saw a blinding white light and felt a "hot flash," he was taking medication containing belladonna, a drug which is psychoactive and produces hallucinations in some patients. White chronicles in some detail also Bill W.'s later experimentation with LSD (which was then a legal and even respectable drug thought to have miraculous properties) in an effort to replicate his religious conversion flash. It was also believed that use of LSD worked to break down AA-aversion among resistant drunks. (One patient is quoted as saying after an LSD trip, "I now find I understand the AA program."!) And much else. But these are just small sidelights to the main story, which proceeds in a predictable, conventional manner. Wilson emerges here neither as devil nor saint but as a rather likeable, self-effacing human, surely a towering figure in the cultural history of the United States, and indirectly, as White shows later, in its politics as well.

White touches all the bases of AA's early history in a readable and useful if not novel way. The real reason to read White is in his extended discussion of the historic interplay between AA and the treatment industry. White has worked as an addiction treatment counselor or in related capacities for the past thirty years, and lived through this history himself. At the core of the dialectic is AA's tradition of anonymity. As the early AA members became involved in the worthy cause of helping to set up hospital facilities for drying out, there developed what White calls the "Knickerbocker Paradox." This refers to a small hospital wing of the 1940s which was set up with AA money, staffed by AA members, whose patients came in entirely via AA referrals, and who could only leave if checked out by AA sponsors. Yet it was forbidden to refer to Knickerbocker as an AA institution. In the public eye, it was completely independent and no AA connection was ever publicly admitted.

Now take this microcosm and fast forward twenty years to the election of Lyndon Baines Johnson and the commencement of the "War on Poverty." LBJ, since 1948 a member of the National Council on Alcoholism (another Knickerbocker-style "independent" body), shepherded through Congress a number of huge appropriation bills and set up a triad of major federal agencies devoted to alcoholism and drug addiction research, policy formulation, and treatment (NIAAA, NIMH and NIDA). With boomlike suddenness, there emerged on the scene what even its benevolent godfather, recovered alcoholic (and undoubtedly AA member) Sen. Harold Hughes later referred to as "the alcoholism and drug abuse industrial complex." In the same political climate, the insurance industry (led by James Kemper, a recovered alcoholic and head of Kemper Insurance) gradually dropped its systematic discrimination against alcoholics and, prodded by the AMA's proclamation of alcoholism as a disease, began underwriting alcoholism and addiction treatment. White quite rightly calls this the "critical center upon which the entire modern industry of addiction treatment has turned." This sudden opening of the public and private purses for alcoholism and addiction treatment led to an "explosive growth" in the treatment industry in the 1960s and 70s. This was a historic victory, as White rightly points out, for the "invisible army" -- the legions of anonymous foot soldiers (and, we should add, many of much higher rank) who had been trained to do the work of AA without using the AA name. It was Knickerbocker writ huge.

Rich in significant detail, White's work affords insights into nonprofit mega-institutes like Hazelden and Lutheran General and others, where millions in public funds went to subsidize and disseminate a treatment philosophy (the Minnesota Model) that has religious conversion and referral to AA as one of its components. And his light also illuminates the for-profit recovery industry, in which the higher operatives pocketed and pocket millions, processing alcoholics as a crop to be harvested for profit; and this, too, although White refrains from saying so, is just another variant of the Knickerbocker paradigm.

But this was not the end of the dialectic of anonymity. The "Knickerbocker Paradox" plainly required the participants to wear two hats, their "AA" hat and their "independent" hat. To put it less charitably, it required them to deny who and what they really were. Massive and widespread role confusion was the result. White speaks in vivid detail of the institutional leaders who attempted, strenuously but often in vain, to clarify for the counseling staff what was "AA work" and what was "counseling work," what they were supposed to give away and what they were being paid for. Numerous and tragic have been the relapses among the army of confused, unsupervised, overworked and underpaid 12-Step "professionals by experience" who were inducted as the corporals and sergeants of the new treatment juggernaut.

The inexorable demand for an institutional program that was definable and replicable (hence insurable and bankable) meant that the 12 Steps, initially sketched as a suggested path of personal spiritual transformation, became transmogrified and blenderized into a compulsory top-down treatment protocol. It was a great victory for the invisible army, but it turned the legions of America's alcoholics and addicts, and many who were neither but happened to be caught in a urine test, into dispirited prisoners of war.

When Knickerbocker was just a small wing of a single hospital, it must have seemed clever to the small guerrilla band of inspired volunteers that all the patients were channeled straight to AA meetings on their release. Today, when virtually every hospital, treatment center, court and prison mandates AA referral, the result is that many AA meetings are overrun "by a growing assortment of sullen, recalcitrant men and women mandated to attend AA meetings by their employers, judges and probation and parole officers," who outnumber the core members by two or three to one on a given night (p. 278). I have heard other informal estimates that put the number of what I am calling "POW members" of AA at more than 70 per cent of the current AA membership. It is not uncommon to hear AA members complain that AA has lost its soul. White cites one such effort, by the widely respected AA historian Ernest Kurtz, to recover "the real AA."

And the story continues. For just as the burgeoning "inebriate asylums" of the 1870s were suddenly swept away by the advent of Prohibition, the "recovery boom" of the 60s and 70s gave way, around the middle 80s, to the Reagan backlash.

Where LBJ had publicly pronounced addiction a disease, the Reagan rhetoric returned the pendulum toward criminalization. Fueled by popular works that challenged the central assumptions of the recovery boom (Fingarette, Peele), and by law-and-order rhetoric, and by the excesses of the movement itself, the right-wing ascendancy began tightening the public purse strings. The "managed care" movement effected the same constriction in the private sector. After taking a cold hard look at what was really being accomplished, insurance companies virtually stopped paying for inpatient treatment, the most lucrative sector of the industry. Today, the recovery boom has gone, or is going, bust. Just as the anonymous footsoldiers of the modern Knickerbocker juggernaut were achieving a measure of professional status and salary, many of them received their pink slips. In 1998, the number of treatment opportunities of any kind available to alcoholics, other than those with private means, is much smaller than two decades ago and continues to constrict. Poorer addicts and minorities, especially, are much more likely today than two decades ago to be sent to jail rather than to any kind of treatment.

Highly worth reading also are White's chapters on the origins of what is called the "modern alcoholism movement." I will just sketch this briefly. After the repeal of Prohibition in 1933, the bloodied and beaten "Drys" sought for a new paradigm. Out of their severe financial crisis emerged what is called "Bowman's compromise," which dropped the traditional barrage against "alcohol" in favor of concern with "alcoholism." The problem was redefined; it no longer lay in the bottle but in the man. White fearlessly cites mounting evidence that alcohol industry money was one of the inducements and one of the rewards for this paradigm shift. One of the most influential institutions in shaping and disseminating what became the Minnesota Model, the summer schools of the Yale Institute of Alcohol Studies, was funded by liquor industry money. In White's words, "The industry saw Alcoholics Anonymous as a potential ally because the organization focused on a small percentage of late-stage drinkers and had little to say about the drinking habits of most Americans. ... AA located the problem of alcohol in the person, not in the bottle." (p. 195). White notes that liquor industry representatives sat on national and local alcoholism councils across the country -- bodies that were typically "Knickerbocker"-style extensions of AA. A careful historian, White notes that evidence about the extent of liquor industry involvement in the modern alcoholism movement is still very scanty. His discussion of the problem is nuanced, detailed, cautious, and never degenerates into sloganeering. There is an illuminating discussion of the ethical and credibility issues involved in liquor industry sponsorship of alcoholism research, although more could be said.

Aficionados of the "disease theory" debate will find this work an invaluable reference. I pointed earlier to the revolutionary doctor Benjamin Rush's pioneering insights, and touched on the first wave of institutional efforts to treat alcoholism as a disease, namely the turn-of-the-century inebriate asylums and the Keeley Institutes. White's well-documented history absolutely obliterates the fallacy that the disease theory was invented by AA. White also quotes both William Miller and Ernest Kurtz, surely authorities on the history of AA, as categorically rejecting any claim that the origin of the disease concept is to be found in AA. According to White, the original AA conceptualization of alcoholism is "emotional and spiritual maladjustment." When AA did use medical terminology, it was "primarily for their metaphoric value -- more for sense-making than for science."

That having been said, however, there is no doubt that AA later became, and is today, perhaps inextricably interwoven with the disease concept in the public mind and perhaps in its own mind as well. The principal weaver of these threads was the indomitable Marty Mann, the first woman to attribute her recovery to AA. Sponsored by the Yale Institute and promoted by AA, she tirelessly crisscrossed the country making thousands of speeches popularizing the disease concept. She portrayed the alcoholic not as a bad person who should be punished but as a good person who was sick and could be helped. What White adds to this story is strong evidence that Mann's presentation ran far ahead of anything that scientific research at that time could support; indeed Dr. Tiebout, one of the seminal thinkers of AA, reflected in 1955 that he trembled to think "how little we have to back up our claims. We are all skating on pretty thin ice." There is much other material as well on several sides of the question in White's account; one comes to the disease debate only half-armed if one has not read this volume.

The reader might think from the foregoing review that William White's book is in some way an expose or indictment of Alcoholics Anonymous. Nothing could be further from the truth. White only presents the "dots," the lines between them are mostly mine. Apart from some rather veiled passages possibly revealing inner doubts, White is 100 per cent "with the program." I would surmise that his own views on recovery are of the amorphous but intense religious kind that is often called "spiritual" for want of a better word. He introduces the hugely revealing "Knickerbocker Paradox" without a hint of negativity. His chapter on the AA program is a bland and one-dimensional recitation of the usual happyface psychological doubletalk. There is not a hint of awareness here that the supposed autonomy of the post-conversion personality can be as much a fiction as was the independence of the Knickerbocker alky ward. He recites the views of various AA critics only for the sake of historical completeness, and without a trace of sympathy. He avoids any direct answer to the question posed by Bill Wilson at AA's 30th anniversary: "What happened to the six hundred thousand who approached

Jean Kirkpatrick, founder of Women for Sobriety

AA and left?" He does not discuss AA's own membership surveys of the 1980s. He does not point out that AA prohibits scientific studies of its effectiveness in promoting recovery. He draws a veil of silence over the rather huge question of the outcome of AA participation, and finds surprising the recent Project Match result that there was no substantial difference in outcomes between 12-Step facilitation and secular treatment modalities. There is an obvious myopia in this area, or perhaps a failure of courage. But this is a minor and not uncommon defect in the book's character. AA, in any event, is only one part of this encyclopedic volume. There are excellent vignettes on many other programs and individuals in the panorama of the modern recovery movement, including Synanon, the Nation of Islam, Glide Memorial, the codependence movements, Women for Sobriety, and many others.

The great strengths of this book are two. One, an obvious thirst for and delight in the raw material of historical evidence. This is a writer who loves historical fact and has an eye for the significant quote and anecdote. This is a rich tapestry that rewards many return trips. And at 390 full-size pages, you get a lot for your money. There's even a section of fine photographs in the middle (sampled here).

Two, the man is honest. There shines through his writing an emotional directness and "there-ness" that is the mark of the very best people I have met in addiction treatment and recovery, or anywhere. I said at the outset that he is quotable. I should add that he can be eloquent when he speaks about what he knows best, the life of the addiction treatment counselor. His ending sounds like a commencement speech at a counselor school, but a moving one. Here are some excerpts from his final words:

> As a culture, we have heaped pleas, profanity, prayers, punishment, and all manner of professional manipulations on the alcoholic and addict, often with little result. With our two centuries of accumulated knowledge and the best available treatments, there still exists no cure for addiction, and only a minority of addicted clients achieve sustained recovery following our intervention in their lives. ... Given this perspective, addiction professionals who claim universal superiority for their treatment disqualify themselves as scientists and healers by the very grandiosity of that claim. The meager results of our best efforts -- along with our history of doing harm in the name of good -- calls for us to approach each client, family and community with respect, humility,

and a devotion to the ultimate principle of ethical practice, 'First, do no harm.'

I also liked very much this passage from his last page, where he tries to formulate in a sentence or two the accumulated therapeutic wisdom of the counseling profession as he understands it. It expresses beautifully something that our LifeRing Handbook also tries to say in our own vocabulary:

> Above all, recognize that what addiction professionals have done for more than a century and a half is to create a setting and an opening in which the addicted can transform their identity and redefine every relationship in their lives, including their relationship with alcohol and other drugs. What we are professionally responsible for is creating a milieu of opportunity, choice and hope. What happens with that opportunity is up to the addict and his or her god. We can own neither the addiction nor the recovery, only the clarity of the presented choice, the best clinical technology we can muster, and our faith in the potential for human rebirth.

That's well said. It expresses with great lucidity the same idea as Dr. Ruth Herman's manifesto-like thesis that each person "must be the author and arbiter of her own recovery." The job of the self-help organization is not to try to fix the person, not to try to own the person or their recovery, but to "create a setting and an opening in which the addicted can transform" themselves -- ourselves.

-- Marty N.

[This review essay originally appeared in the BookTalk section on www.unhooked.com. It has been modified for this volume.]

Where Does the LifeRing Recovery Approach Fit Within the Spectrum of Contemporary Treatment Methods?

(Review of Reid K. Hester, William R. Miller, editors: *Handbook of Alcoholism Treatment Approaches: Effective Alternatives.* 2nd Ed. Allyn & Bacon, 1995. ISBN 0205163769.)

The editors and authors of this *Handbook of Alcoholism Treatment Approaches* set themselves the task of comparing the variety of treatment approaches in the alcoholism field to see which ones are more effective than others. Toward this end, they excluded studies that consist basically of anecdotal evidence and included only studies that used a control or comparison group -- the same basic method used in all scientific research. They reviewed some 211 published studies meeting this criterion. Their conclusion is one that ought to shake the treatment industry to its foundations: the substance abuse treatment methods that are in the most widespread use today are those for which there is the least scientific evidence of effectiveness. The dominant treatment paradigm has little or no scientific basis and there is much evidence that its most important product is failure. If someone set out to design a system to be as ineffective as possible, it would closely resemble what we have today.

> "The negative correlation between scientific evidence and application in standard practice could hardly be larger if one intentionally constructed treatment programs from those approaches with the *least* evidence of efficacy." (p. 33)

This is an important book worth reading cover to cover. In this review I want first to outline the content of the work, to give the general reader an idea of its findings and arguments. In the

"Confrontational counseling styles have enjoyed particular popularity in U.S. alcoholism treatment. Yet confrontational approaches have failed to yield a single positive outcome study." (p. 27).

second section I will try briefly to draw some lessons from the work for the theory and practice of our alternative self-help recovery organization.

The authors classify the variety of current treatment approaches into eleven broad types. Based on the outcomes of the published controlled studies, they rank these modalities from the most effective to the least effective as follows:

Methods that have consistently positive or mixed but predominantly positive outcome studies: brief intervention; broad-spectrum skills training; marital/family therapy; cognitive-behavioral methods, and aversion therapies.

Methods with equivocal results: Antabuse and psychoactive drugs.

Methods with consistently or predominantly negative outcome studies: Psychotherapies. Confrontational methods.

And finally, lowest on the ladder of scientifically demonstrated effectiveness, the so-called standard methods used almost universally in the US treatment industry.
The standard approach used in the US treatment industry is the "Minnesota Model." This "generic" approach consists of the 12 Steps of Alcoholics Anonymous augmented by group psychotherapy, educational lectures and films, and counseling, frequently of a confrontational nature. Controlled studies of this approach almost universally fail to find any advantage over untreated or alternatively treated groups. Yet this approach is unquestionably the foundation of the standard treatment model in the United States.

As the authors note, in the US treatment industry today there is an enormous gap between science and practice. If one had

> **"There is no tried and true, 'state-of-the-art' treatment of choice for alcohol problems. Rather, the state of the art is an array of empirically supported treatment options." (p. 9)**

deliberately designed the treatment industry to be as ineffective as possible, one would have created the present system.

The conclusion the authors draw from their survey of different treatment methods is that no one approach -- least of all the dominant Minnesota Model -- is likely to be effective for most alcoholics.   The basic assumption of the dominant paradigm, that all alcoholics should be treated the same way, is fundamentally flawed. The authors' objective is to move treatment away from a single model, "operating as if it were the only complete and accurate understanding of alcohol problems and their etiology," toward "a range of effective alternatives." (p. 8). They wish to present the clinician, and thus ultimately the patient, with "a variety of promising tools to use in working with different types of alcohol problems and individuals." (p. 8).

The editors call their strategy "informed eclecticism." Informed eclecticism seeks a position beyond the hollow dogmatism that only one method works, and also beyond the naïve optimism that everything works equally well.   The clinician's attitude should be one of openness to a variety of approaches, guided by scientific evidence. Four principles are basic to informed eclecticism:

(1) No single approach to treatment is superior for all individuals. The "state of the art" is not a single method, but "an array of empirically supported treatment options."

(2) Treatment programs should offer a variety of different treatment approaches. The program should have a menu of options.

> "Although Alcoholics Anonymous (AA) is widely recommended by U.S. treatment programs, its efficacy has rarely been studied [....] Only two controlled trials were found in which AA was studied as a distinct alternative, both with offender populations required to attend AA or other conditions, and both finding no beneficial effect." (p. 31).

(3) Different types of people respond best to different approaches.

(4) The art of the clinician lies in matching the right treatment to the right patient the first time around. Doing so increases efficacy, avoids waste, and improves staff morale.

The authors are keenly aware that there are many obstacles in the way of their approach. Existing treatment programs show almost no real variety and alternatives are almost absent. They write that their own community (Albuquerque) has more than 50 different programs, but most of them are "virtual carbon copies of one another." (p. 9). Clear criteria for distinguishing among types of patients and for matching treatment to patient remain to be developed. Irrational motives, economic forces, and institutional inertia often override the patient's best interest. People doing intake and patient evaluation are often the least trained staff members, and frequently have blinding biases toward the particular approach that worked for them.

The client's welfare ought to be the overriding criterion. "It is clear that inappropriately matched clients can be harmed, faring worse than if they had received no treatment at all. Individuals matched to the right treatment the first time can be spared years of needless suffering and impairment. A common concern for those who suffer from alcohol problems should, in the end, be the most persuasive ground for agreement and cooperation toward a comprehensive system of informed eclecticism." (p. 10)

After the groundbreaking introductory chapters, the Hester/Miller handbook settles down and presents what amounts to a training manual for clinicians, from screening methods and intake procedures through the various supported modalities of treatment and ending with post-treatment follow-up and evaluation. Here are some of the highlights that caught my eye.

The chapter on evaluation of alcohol problems by Miller, Westerberg & Waldron examines some of the basic measurement technology used in the treatment industry and finds it wanting. The authors remark that a diagnosis of "alcoholism" was once considered sufficient to commence treatment. But now "a more complex contemporary understanding has evolved" which sees many degrees and shades of alcohol problems. Specific tests have evolved to detect and measure these varieties. However, those instruments that have scientific evidence to support their efficacy are very little used, whereas the tests and checklists in common use have little or no scientific underpinnings.

Like diagnosis, evaluation of program efficacy is rarely done in a conscientious manner, or at all. When outcomes are studied, it is sometimes found that programs believed to be effective actually increase rather than decrease the problem. Outcome studies also torpedoed another cherished belief of the treatment industry, namely that expensive inpatient care is more effective than the much cheaper outpatient treatment (p. 81). Indeed, the editors consistently found an inverse correlation between treatment cost and evidence of efficacy (p. 13).

The authors are too polite to say so but one conclusion that can be drawn from this chapter is that the standard model of alcoholism treatment in this country operates basically with its eyes closed. It knows neither what it is doing nor what it has done.

An outstanding chapter is the contribution of William R. Miller titled "Increasing Motivation for Change." Everyone agrees that client motivation is a key issue in recovery. But there the agreement stops. In the traditional view, motivation or the lack of it ("denial") is rooted in the alcoholic's character

> "A strong and consistent finding in research on motivation is that people are most likely to undertake and persist in an action when they perceive that they have personally chosen to do so. One study, for example, found that a particular alcohol treatment approach was more effective when a client chose it from among alternatives than when it was assigned to the client as his or her only option . [...] Perceived freedom of choice also appears to reduce client resistance and dropout [....] When clients are told they have no choice, they tend to resist change. When their freedom of choice is acknowledged, they are freed to choose change." (p. 93).

structure or personality. Only when that structure is shattered by some disastrous event ("hitting bottom") or when divine intervention removes its defects can motivation to get sober emerge.

Yet in the past 30 years this paradigm has begun to crack. Several findings contributed to undermine it. More alcoholics became sober before landing in the gutter, and the idea arose that it might be possible to "raise the bottom" by appropriate intervention. It was also recognized that the alcoholic's social environment was frequently intertwined with the problem, and that changes in the environment produced changes in motivation. Another nail in the coffin of the "character" paradigm of motivation was the accumulation of negative findings concerning an "alcoholic personality." Finally, studies comparing different treatment styles and personalities found that some counselors were very effective in motivating clients to complete treatment, whereas others "lost" a high proportion of their patients. Studies showed that a small number of staff members in a given center produced the great majority of patient dropouts. The evidence is that patient motivation is not so much a factor of the patient's personality as of the counselor's.

The new approach to client motivation is that patient motivation is not found but made. The therapist need not wait for the drinker to "hit bottom" -- or, worse, encourage the patient's descent. The therapist, according to Miller, has many tools available to enhance the client's motivation, and a large part of the professional's skill consists in using them effectively and in a timely manner. Based on hundreds of research studies examining various approaches to enhancing client motivation, Miller identifies six common elements of an effective motivational toolkit. They are:

Personal feedback. Studies showed that drinkers who were given live personal feedback about their drinking situation, even very briefly, did significantly better than those who merely heard lectures or saw films.

Personal responsibility. Because this is such an important element in the self-help process I want to quote the author at some length.

"A second common element in effective motivational intervention is an emphasis on the client's personal responsibility and freedom of choice. Rather than giving

"Fifty years of both psychological [...] and longitudinal studies [...] have failed to reveal a consistent 'alcoholic personality.' Attempts to derive a set of alcoholic psychometric personality subtypes have yielded profiles similar to those found when subtyping a general population [...]. That is, alcoholics appear to be as variable in personality as are nonalcoholics.

Studies of character defense mechanisms among alcoholics have yielded a similar picture. Denial and other defense mechanisms have been found to be no more nor less frequent among alcoholics than among people in general. [...] There was simply no support for the view that alcoholics in general come into treatment with a consistent set of personality traits and defenses." (p. 90) restrictive messages (You have to, can't, must, etc.), the counselor acknowledges that ultimately it is up to the client whether or not to change: 'No one can change your drinking for you, or make you change. It's really up to you. You can choose to keep on drinking as you have been. You can choose to make a change. Even if I wanted to, I can't decide this for you.' In addition to being therapeutic, this message is quite simply the truth. A therapist cannot alter the client's ultimate personal responsibility and choice.

"Why is this message helpful in triggering change? A strong and consistent finding in research on motivation is that people are most likely to undertake and persist in an action when they perceive that they have personally chosen to do so. One study, for example, found that a particular alcohol treatment approach was more effective when a client chose it from among alternatives than when it was assigned to the client as his or her only option . [...] Perceived freedom of choice also appears to reduce client resistance and dropout [....] When clients are told they have no choice, they tend to resist change. When their freedom of choice is acknowledged, they are freed to choose change." (p. 93).

Advice. A simple and effective method is for the treatment professional, typically a physician, to advise the patient to act.

Real Choice. It is pointless for the therapist to try to mobilize the client's personal responsibility unless there are actually alternatives available for the client to choose from. The counseling methods that work most effectively are those that offer a real choice for the patient to make. The key is to get the client "actively involved in choosing his or her own approach." (p. 94).

Empathy. Studies show that the most effective counselors are those who maintain a client-centered approach. They are felt to be warm, supportive, sympathetic and attentive. Counselors who have these qualities are effective regardless of whether they are themselves persons in recovery. By contrast, counselors with a confrontational, harsh, or punitive style tend to score poorly in long-term outcome studies.

Hope. Motivation ultimately depends on the client's belief that improvement is possible, that is, on the ignition of hope. Fear of negative consequences -- the mainstay of the traditional methods -- is rarely sufficient. There must be a belief that it is within the client's power to change.

> "There is also reason to believe that clients have wisdom about what is most likely to work for them." (p. 100)

Miller and his colleagues have attempted to assemble these elements into a treatment program they call Motivational Interviewing. The basic idea of this approach is to facilitate the client's inner struggle between addiction and recovery and to empower the client's own healthy resources. Toward that end, the counselor encourages the client to select and to construct a personal treatment plan, because research shows the unsurprising fact that "clients tend to be more committed to a plan that they perceive as their own, addressing personal concerns." (p. 95). "[R]esearch suggests that treatments chosen by a client from among alternatives are more likely to be adhered to and effective. The choice process increases the client's perception of personal control and enhances motivation for compliance. ... [I]ndividualized strategies lead to increased positive outcomes." (p. 100). Indeed, Miller goes so far as to say: "There is also reason to believe that clients have wisdom about what is most likely to work for them."

An authoritarian approach by the therapist typically backfires. Miller argues persuasively that client "denial" in the treatment setting is unnecessary and is primarily the result of hapless therapy.

A prominent example is the issue whether or not the client must accept the label of "alcoholic." Treatment programs modeled on the first step of Alcoholics Anonymous often begin with a power struggle between client and therapist over acceptance of the "alcoholic" label. Miller says that research finds no strong relationship between self-labeling and outcome. "Many treatment failures are quite willing to accept the label 'alcoholic,' and many people respond favorably to treatment without ever calling themselves alcoholic." (p. 95). The principal outcome of this traditional power struggle is the counterproductive one of mobilizing the client's denial and entrenching resistance. It would appear that the seeds of failure in the standard model treatment program are frequently planted with the very first step.

Closely related to Miller's important chapter on motivation is the chapter on Relapse Prevention by Linda Dimeff and G. Alan Marlatt. This begins with the memorable words: "The most common treatment outcome for alcoholics and addicts is relapse." (p. 176). After everything that has been said before, this should not be surprising. Since the standard paradigm of the treatment industry lacks scientific validation and consists almost entirely of tools and modalities that are demonstrably ineffective if not counterproductive, it would be astonishing if the primary product of the process were anything but failure.

> **Relapse prevention "is most successful when the client confidently acts as his or her own therapist following treatment." (p. 177)**

The only dispute is about the magnitude of the debacle. Relapse figures run from about two thirds at 90 days (p. 176) to more than 90 per cent over longer periods (p. 92). The only astonishing thing about these numbers is that there is not more of a public outcry for reform of the industry.

I will not try to summarize the Dimeff/Marlatt Relapse Prevention approach in any detail. The key theme is that clients are most successful at avoiding relapse if they emerge from treatment empowered and equipped to heal themselves, rather than dependent on some outside contingency. In the authors' words, relapse prevention "is most successful when the client confidently acts as his or her own therapist following treatment." (p. 177). The client best avoids relapse when he or she is viewed as the rightful agent of change. Client motivation, largely a function of self-determination in choosing the treatment methods, is key, as is equipping the client "with the necessary skills to act as his or her own future therapist." (p. 178). The approach works best when "tailored to the individual." (192).

There are a number of other chapters that explore treatment alternatives to the standard paradigm. I will not take the space to discuss them here. However, at some point the gist of these chapters should be added to the LifeRing sobriety toolkit (Handbook of Secular Recovery, Ch. IV) and made more widely available to our readership.

What does the Hester/Miller Handbook teach us about the place of the LifeRing S.R. approach in the spectrum of contemporary treatment modalities?

First of all, the book validates the feeling that so many of our members have had, that the standard 12-Step-based treatment programs which they were forced to endure were ineffective at best and counterproductive in many cases. So many who participate in our groups report that they managed to stay sober despite their treatment program, not because of it. The Hester/Miller book supplies evidence and explanations to corroborate the private pain that many felt and still feel from this experience.

Secondly, the publication of this book, and the number and prominence of its contributors, is further evidence that the ruling paradigm is eroding. The editors and authors include a number of prominent and well-placed senior names in university, clinical and government settings, as well as young graduate students joining the ranks (see endnote).
The book confirms what the experience of our LifeRing Secular Recovery groups in the San Francisco Bay Area in the past few years has demonstrated. More and more treatment programs exist that really care about what works, that are open-minded, that allow their methods to be influenced by scientific research, and that believe in offering their clients a choice of support groups.

The **third** conclusion I draw from the Hester/Miller Handbook is that the LifeRing S.R. approach to the central therapeutic issues of recovery is a sound and forward-looking one.

Our own Handbook (*Handbook of Secular Recovery*, LifeRing Press 1999) advocates an individualized, constructivist approach that maximizes the recovering person's own motivation. We say that each recovering alcoholic has the ability, with group support, to develop a personalized recovery plan that works for that individual. We say that each person has the wisdom to do this. We say that when people develop their own recovery plans, they are more deeply committed to their recovery. We say that when people are encouraged to act as their own therapist, they can more readily modify their program to meet contingencies and they will better resist relapse.

All of these points, which our own Handbook merely asserts in the form of a manifesto, find corroboration in the Hester/Miller Handbook. Published research with controlled trials demonstrates that the cardinal therapeutic principles of the LifeRing S.R. approach are valid and effective ones. Hester and Miller's "enlightened eclecticism" is a good description of the principles of choice and diversity of treatment tools that we so eminently embody.

Reid Hester is director of an alcoholism clinic and a research associate professor at the University of New Mexico. William R. Miller is professor of psychology and psychiatry at the University of New Mexico. Among the contributing authors are prominent academics, clinicians and treatment administrators, including Prof. David Abrams of Brown University, John Allen, chief of the Treatment Research Branch of the National Institute on Alcohol Abuse and Alcoholism, Ned Cooney, director of the VA Medical Center in New Haven, Prof. Richard Frances, the chair of the Council on Addiction Psychiatry of the American Psychiatric Association, Richard K. Fuller, director of Research at the National Institute of Alcohol Abuse and Alcoholism, Prof. G.

Alan Marlatt, director of the Addictive Behaviors Research Center at the University of Washington, Prof. Sheldon I. Miller, chair of the department of psychiatry at Northwestern University Medical School, Lisa Rone, chief resident in psychiatry at Northwestern Memorial Hospital in Chicago, and others.

-- Marty N.

[This review essay previously appeared in the BookTalk section on www.unhooked.com, and has been modified for this volume.]

[Notes]

A Clinical Protocol Based on the Sober Self-Empowerment Concept

(Review of *You Can Free Yourself From Alcohol and Drugs: Work a Program That Keeps You in Charge*, by Doug Althauser, M.Ed., CSAC, MAC. Oakland: New Harbinger Publications, 1998. ISBN 1-57224-118-7.)

Kaiser Permanente is the largest Health Maintenance Organization in the United States, and practically all of its centers include Chemical Dependency Recovery Programs (CDRP). When the Program Coordinator of one of these CDRPs writes a book about recovery, it pays to sit up and listen. Doug Althauser is Program Coordinator of the CDRP at Kaiser in Honolulu. His book, based on nearly ten years of clinical experience, is a fascinating effort to move beyond the old spiritual paradigm of the 12 Steps into a newer, more secular and more self-empowering recovery model. The book is of special interest to LifeRing members because many of its themes resonate with our own concerns.

In the Introduction to this book, Althauser makes the following historical observation:

> In the 1970s, the culture of North America changed. People became less likely to discuss God or spirituality in informal group settings like AA or NA meetings. Furthermore, people began to express pride over their individual characteristics, like their culture, their gender, race, ethnicity, or personal philosophy. This independence made it tough for a lot of addicts and alcoholics to accept the spiritual philosophy of Twelve-Step programs. Not surprisingly, chemically dependent people began to ask for alternatives to the Twelve Steps. As a result, three different groups began on a national level helping people to recover: Women for Sobriety, Secular Organizations for

Sobriety (or Save Our Selves), and Rational Recovery. These groups provided an alternative to Twelve-Step programs. More importantly, these alternative programs worked.

(p. 2). Althauser's clinical practice has led him to construct a recovery program that is better adapted to this newer, less traditionally spiritual, more diverse, and more proudly independent recovering population, and that has a higher appreciation of the alternative support groups.

What all different kinds of recovery approaches have in common, he says, is three basic things: (1) abstinence as a lifelong goal; (2) changes in lifestyle to minimize risks of relapse; and (3) use of a support group of some kind to maintain sobriety over time. When he says "of some kind," Althauser really means it. He recognizes that the 12-Step groups are much more widely available than the alternatives, but he intends his program to be compatible with any kind of group that helps a person stay abstinent, regardless of its ideology. He regards all such groups as more or less equally valid and helpful, and specifically includes LifeRing's predecessor (SOS).

When Althauser begins to detail his program, it may seem at first sight that this is another in the long series of attempts to make the 12-Step program palatable by selectively ignoring and sugar-coating what it actually says. Thus, Althauser's program consists of "Ten Goals" that must be done in order, like steps. The first goal is to admit that one is chemically dependent, somewhat like the First Step; and each of the subsequent goals is similarly developed via a brief interpretation of the corresponding points in the 12-Step program. On the surface this looks at first like another 12-Step clone.

But this appearance deceives. Althauser's project is to extract from the Steps what he sees as "the therapeutic, that is, the non-spiritual recovery concepts" and to leave the rest behind. His effort, in his words, is to use from the 12 Steps only "the parts that work for everyone." He advises at the outset that his program is not a 12-Step program, that it has nothing to do with any 12-Step groups, and that 12-Step groups neither asked for the book to be written nor reviewed or approved it in any way.

Central to the Steps is "God" and a "Power greater than ourselves." Althauser handles this issue by translating all such references into the concept of "sources of support." These sources, he says, need not be "powers greater than oneself" but merely people one can trust to help one stay abstinent. He has no problem with clients who include God in their list of sources of support, but he advises that only people who can give you direct feedback can really be effective for you. So, for example, the list "God, Jesus, Holy Spirit, Virgin Mary, Saint Mary Magdalena, my rosary, my priest, the Pope, the Bible and my church" contains only one possibly effective source of support, the priest, and he is probably too unavailable to give much feedback. The patient who made this particular list, Althauser recounts, soon relapsed.

Althauser's approach throughout is informed with clinical experience and inspired by common sense. There is a good array of checklists to help a patient decide whether a self-diagnosis of chemical dependency is warranted. There is an excellent chapter on why abstinence is the appropriate lifetime goal. There is a wealth of good advice about high-risk and lower-risk lifestyle choices. Althauser wisely advises leaving deep psychological self-examination aside during early sobriety and focusing instead on examining one's everyday behavior patterns. He gives numerous anecdotes to illustrate healthy and unhealthy lifestyle decisions among his patients. This book is a good compendium of sound information and advice for living sober.

At the center of Althauser's program (around goal six) is "drafting your own sobriety plan." The plan is based on two lists: a list of one's high-risk lifestyle elements and a list of the elements in one's current life that help one maintain abstinence. The plan consists of detailed, specific actions that move away from the relapse-prone toward the more securely abstinent behaviors. Relapse or near-relapse is simply a sign that the program needs to be revised. Althauser emphasizes that each person's plan must be based on that person's actual individual life situation, and cannot be simply copied from a formula in a book. Althauser expressly recognizes that this individualized approach will result in a group whose members will have different sobriety plans. This diversity – perceived as threatening in traditional programs, where therapeutic uniformity is the goal -- is actually a sign that the program is working, and is a source of its strength.

This book may be particularly useful to that large number of early recovering people who are treading in 12-step waters without any real sense of direction. The book extends a branch to them by which they can pull themselves up to some solid therapeutic ground. The book belongs in every LifeRing member's recovery library. It would make a good gift for a person newly embarking on the recovery path or a person still drinking but actively contemplating a change.

There are some weaknesses. Althauser contends at several points that his program captures the "real meaning" of the Steps by interpreting the words as they were understood when written in 1935. This effort is based on nothing more than a 1934 edition of the New Century Dictionary, and it isn't particularly persuasive. Also, to someone like myself who has had the privilege of doing all my recovery in LifeRing (formerly SOS), Althauser's continuous effort to explain his program in terms of the 12-Step framework appears unnecessary and counterproductive, sometimes annoyingly so. I find myself wishing sometimes he would just "kick out the jams" and say what he means to say without trying to harmonize it first with the 12-Step viewpoint. But I can very well understand why someone in charge of a major treatment program in this day and age would still find it necessary to jump through that series of hoops.

In my view this book is an important one for LifeRing members. To my eyes there are two main lessons here. One is that the secular, do-it-yourself-with-group-support approach that LifeRing espouses is finding more and more echoes within the walls of the professional treatment community.

What was once a closed shop where only 12-step groups need apply for recognition is opening up, little by little, to acknowledge the validity of alternative approaches, including LifeRing.

Althauser's program, at its core, is built around the same idea as the LifeRing view, namely that if given the proper support and tools, each motivated recovering person can and will construct the sobriety program that works for that individual. It is gratifying to find prominent voices in the treatment profession who resonate with this important therapeutic idea, central to the LifeRing approach.

The main portion of the book is addressed to persons in recovery. The presentation is clear, respectful of the recovering reader's intelligence, and filled with illustrative anecdotes. The author adds a postscript (Chapter 12) addressed to other treatment professionals. Here, Althauser lets his hair down and explains the "ten goals" in terms that have nothing to do with the 12 Steps but speak the language of cognitive behavioral psychology. There is much practical and strategic material here for staff meeting discussions; really, this last chapter contains the compressed outline of another whole book. I hope Althauser writes that sequel soon.

-- Marty N.

[This review essay previously appeared in the BookTalk section on www.unhooked.com, and has been modified for this volume.]

[Notes]

Through Other Eyes: From the History of LifeRing Secular Recovery

(LifeRing S.R. was formerly known as Secular Organizations for Sobriety (SOS)).

William L. White:

Secular Sobriety Groups – later renamed Secular Organizations for Sobriety – Save Our Selves (SOS) was organized in 1985 by James Christopher, an alcoholic who had achieved sobriety in spite of his frustrations with A.A.'s perceived religious trappings. When he wrote an articles on his struggles as an atheist in A.A., he received responses that convinced him that thousands of alcoholics desired a non-spiritual alternative to A.A. There is much in SOS that bears a striking resemblance to A.A. If one imagined support groups that operate much like A.A., but without references to Higher Power, God, or prayer, one would be very close to a picture of the SOS milieu. SOS places emphasis on the 'sobriety priority,' 'not drinking no matter what,' and on maintaining perpetual vigilance to keep from awakening the 'sleeping giant' of addiction. SOS rejects A.A.'s requirement of personal anonymity at the public level, A.A.'s emphasis on helping other alcoholics as a means of staying sober, and A.A.'s practice of sponsorship. ... [*From: Slaying the Dragon: The History of Addiction Treatment and Recovery in America, by William L. White (p. 280)*]

Charlotte Kasl, Ph.D.:

The core of Christopher's approach to abstinence is his "sobriety priority" statement: "I *don't drink,* no *matter what.* " He separates sobriety from all other problems and believes one always has a choice. Thus he takes the stance, "Even if I'm tired, upset, abandoned, or going crazy, I don't drink no *matter what.* If I go crazy, I will go crazy sober."

From Christopher's observations and research into what keeps alcoholics sober, he has reached the following conclusion: "Alcoholics who practice daily and adhere to their individual sobriety priority no *matter what* stay sober for the long term; the others simply do not, whether or not they believe in God." This coincides with my observations over the years. When I ask people what they say to themselves to keep from using again, I hear statements such as, "If I use, it will kill me . . . I don't ever want to go through withdrawal again. It's not worth it." Essentially, these are sobriety priority statements. This is in sharp contrast to AA's suggestion that one will surely drink if they build up resentments, get tired, and so on. ...

Christopher concurs with research that shows alcoholism to be a physical disease. He believes emphatically that the 10 percent of us whose body chemistry cannot tolerate alcohol must have complete abstinence, making sobriety the number one priority in their lives. Because it is a physical disease, he sees people with this disease as neither morally superior nor inferior to people without the disease, just as people with diabetes or cancer are not morally inferior or superior. Christopher says that character defects do not cause alcoholism, and therefore are not directly related to recovery. Rather, he believes that people often require medical treatment initially in sobriety, and then must adhere to their sobriety priority, which they can do, character defects and all. ...

In accordance with his dislike of indoctrination, Christopher does not like the idea of sponsors. He believes that too often older members of the group inculcate the group practices into new members, who may be extremely vulnerable to any teachings when they are so desperate for sobriety. In *How to Stay Sober,* he discusses his experiences with sponsors, and concludes by saying, "In sobriety I think we'd do well to avoid sponsorship, approaching each other as equals, walking side by side." *[From: Many Roads, One Journey, Moving Beyond the Twelve Steps, by Charlotte Davis Kasl, Ph.D, 1992 (pp. 172-174)]*

Gerard J. Connors, Ph.D., Kurt H. Dermen, Ph.D.:

Self-help groups have assisted many in their recovery from alcohol use disorders. Although Alcoholics Anonymous (AA) is the largest self-help organization for addressing alcohol problems, no single organization can be suited to the needs of all alcohol abusers. For example, some alcoholics have chosen not to affiliate with AA because of objections to religious or spiritual references in the 12 steps of AA. It was largely for this reason that a secular self-help organization—Secular Organizations for Sobriety (SOS)—was established. This article provides an overview of SOS. Also described are the results of a survey of SOS participants. These data provide a preliminary picture of SOS members and will, we hope, stimulate further research on this organization and its effectiveness.

Participation in mutual self-help groups has assisted many in their recovery from alcohol use disorders. Although Alcoholics Anonymous (AA) is the largest and best known of such groups, no one organization can be suited to the needs of all alcohol abusers. Some evidence for this has been the establishment of alternative self-help groups, such as Rational Recovery and Women for Sobriety.

It has been noted that A.A. does not appeal to all alcohol abusers […]. Some, for example, object to the religious and/or spiritual references found in the 12 steps of A.A., which serve as a cornerstone for the organization. These alcoholics feel that A.A. has a religious or spiritual orientation different from their own, or object to any reference to God in the tenets of A.A. Despite the view of many within A.A. that the references to 'a power grater than ourselves' and 'God as we understand him' […] leave participation open to individuals with a wide variety of views on God and religion […], many alcoholics have felt alienated by this aspect. It was largely for this reason that a secular self-help organization – SOS – was established in the United States in 1986.

Since it is a relatively new organization, SOS has been the subject of little empirical study... [This article will] report on the results of a survey of SOS participants [in 1990-91]...

Based on the data from those who responded, the results suggest that SOS is attracting those individuals for whom it originally was conceived.....

The reactions of the SOS members to the organization consistently were positive. Respondents in particular enjoyed the absence of a religious orientation, the SOS content, and the overall atmosphere (including interpersonal factors). Particularly noteworthy was that they found the program useful in achieving and maintaining abstinence from substance use. The majority reported that they were planning long-term affiliation with SOS.

Almost all of the respondents had been exposed to AA. Indeed, the average rate of AA attendance in the previous month was 4.5 meetings. The positive features of AA most often reported revolved around the benefits derived from interpersonal relationships with AA members (such as social support, friendship, and sharing). The majority, however, indicated a dislike for the perceived focus on religion and higher power, and over half reported that they did not anticipate future AA attendance. Nevertheless, the finding that there was this extent of attendance at both SOS and AA was noteworthy. It is possible that the two organizations are viewed by many as being complementary in their relative strengths. In this regard, they might view AA's strengths as its stability and ubiquitous nature and SOS's strength as its freedom from what is perceived by some as dogma regarding the role of God and spirituality. *[From: Characteristics of Participants in Secular Organizations for Sobriety (SOS), by Gerard J. Connors, Ph.D., Kurt H. Dermen, Ph.D., Am J. Drug Alcohol Abuse, 22(2), pp. 281-295 (1996).]*

Principles of Effective Treatment [NIDA]

[From: Principles of Drug Addiction Treatment: A Research-Based Guide, National Institute of Drug Abuse (NIDA), Oct. 1999]

1. **No single treatment is appropriate for all individuals.** Matching treatment settings, interventions, and services to each individual's particular problems and needs is critical to his or her ultimate success in returning to productive functioning in the family, workplace, and society.

2. **Treatment needs to be readily available.** Because individuals who are addicted to drugs may be uncertain about entering treatment, taking advantage of opportunities when they are ready for treatment is crucial. Potential treatment applicants can be lost if treatment is not immediately available or is not readily accessible.

3. **Effective treatment attends to multiple needs of the individual, not just his or her drug use.** To be effective, treatment must address the individual's drug use and any associated medical, psychological, social, vocational, and legal problems.

4. **An individual's treatment and services plan must be assessed continually and modified as necessary to ensure that the plan meets the person's changing needs.** A patient may require varying combinations of services and treatment components during the course of treatment and recovery. In addition to counseling or psychotherapy, a patient at times may require medication, other medical services, family therapy, parenting instruction, vocational rehabilitation, and social and legal services. It is critical that the treatment approach be

appropriate to the individual's age, gender, ethnicity, and culture.

5. **Remaining in treatment for an adequate period of time is critical for treatment effectiveness.** The appropriate duration for an individual depends on his or her problems and needs. Research indicates that for most patients, the threshold of significant improvement is reached at about 3 months in treatment. After this threshold is reached, additional treatment can produce further progress toward recovery. Because people often leave treatment prematurely, programs should include strategies to engage and keep patients in treatment.

6. **Counseling (individual and/or group) and other behavioral therapies are critical components of effective treatment for addiction.** In therapy, patients address issues of motivation, build skills to resist drug use, replace drug-using activities with constructive and rewarding nondrug-using activities, and improve problem-solving abilities. Behavioral therapy also facilitates interpersonal relationships and the individual's ability to function in the family and community. ...

7. **Medications are an important element of treatment for many patients, especially when combined with counseling and other behavioral therapies.** Methadone and levo-alpha-acetylmethadol (LAAM) are very effective in helping individuals addicted to heroin or other opiates stabilize their lives and reduce their illicit drug use. Naltrexone is also an effective medication for some opiate addicts and some patients with co-occurring alcohol dependence. For persons addicted to nicotine, a nicotine replacement product (such as patches or gum) or an oral medication (such as bupropion) can be an effective component of treatment. For patients with mental disorders, both behavioral treatments and medications can be critically important.

8. **Addicted or drug-abusing individuals with coexisting mental disorders should have both disorders treated in an integrated way.** Because addictive disorders and mental disorders often occur in the same individual, patients presenting for either condition should be assessed and treated for the co-occurrence of the other type of disorder.

9. **Medical detoxification is only the first stage of addiction treatment and by itself does little to change long-term drug use.** Medical detoxification safely manages the acute physical symptoms of withdrawal associated with stopping drug use. While detoxification alone is rarely sufficient to help addicts achieve long-term abstinence, for some individuals it is a strongly indicated precursor to effective drug addiction treatment (*see Drug Addiction Treatment Section*).

10. **Treatment does not need to be voluntary to be effective.** Strong motivation can facilitate the treatment process. Sanctions or enticements in the family, employment setting, or criminal justice system can increase significantly both treatment entry and retention rates and the success of drug treatment interventions.

11. **Possible drug use during treatment must be monitored continuously.** Lapses to drug use can occur during treatment. The objective monitoring of a patient's drug and alcohol use during treatment, such as through urinalysis or other tests, can help the patient withstand urges to use drugs. Such monitoring also can provide early evidence of drug use so that the individual's treatment plan can be adjusted. Feedback to patients who test positive for illicit drug use is an important element of monitoring.

12. **Treatment programs should provide assessment for HIV/AIDS, hepatitis B and C, tuberculosis and other infectious diseases, and counseling to help**

patients modify or change behaviors that place themselves or others at risk of infection. Counseling can help patients avoid high-risk behavior. Counseling also can help people who are already infected manage their illness.

13. **Recovery from drug addiction can be a long-term process and frequently requires multiple episodes of treatment.** As with other chronic illnesses, relapses to drug use can occur during or after successful treatment episodes. Addicted individuals may require prolonged treatment and multiple episodes of treatment to achieve long-term abstinence and fully restored functioning. Participation in self-help support programs during and following treatment often is helpful in maintaining abstinence.

Further Reading

Books:

Handbook of Secular Recovery (formerly: *Sobriety Handbook: The SOS Way*). LifeRing Press, edition 1.5, 50 pp., 1999. Available online at www.lifering.com or as an offprint in 8.5x11" format, tape bound. $5.00 & s/h from LifeRing Press.

Keepers: Voices of Secular Recovery. Edited and with an introduction by Marty Nicolaus. 224 pp. paperbound, 5.25x8.5". $12 & s/h from LifeRing Press, 1999. Quantity discounts to LifeRing meetings and institutions. A selection of more than 100 motivational short items about sobriety, secularity and self-help culled from Tom Shelley's secular sobriety email list, 1996-1999. Includes Holiday Survival Guide. Order from LifeRing Press.

My Personal Recovery Program: A Workbook. Forthcoming from LifeRing Press. 8.5x11", 120+ pp. A comprehensive open-ended tool for writing one's own recovery plan. Available Fall 2000. Order from LifeRing Press.

The Secular Prisoner Book. Forthcoming from LifeRing Press. An annotated collection of recent appeals court cases holding that AA-NA programs are "religious" within the meaning of the First Amendment of the federal Constitution, and that prisoners may not be compelled to attend them unless a secular alternative is made available on an equal footing. With prisoner stories and how-to guides for compliance with the court mandates. Available late 2000. Order from LifeRing Press.

Slaying the Dragon: The History of Addiction Treatment and Recovery in America, by William L. White (1998) Chestnut Health Systems / Lighthouse Institute, ISBN 0-938475-07-X ($19.95). Reviewed in this volume. Order from any bookstore.

Handbook of Alcoholism Treatment Approaches: Effective Alternatives. Reid K. Hester, William R. Miller, editors. 2nd Ed. Allyn & Bacon, 1995. ISBN 0205163769. ($56.95) Reviewed in this volume. Order from any bookstore.

You Can Free Yourself From Alcohol and Drugs: Work a Program That Keeps You in Charge, by Doug Althauser, M.Ed., CSAC, MAC. Oakland: New Harbinger Publications, 1998. ISBN 1-57224-118-7. Reviewed in this volume. Order from any bookstore.

SOS Sobriety: The Proven Alternative to 12-Step Programs, by James Christopher (Prometheus Press, 1992). 240 pages, $15.95. Prometheus Press N.Y. 1992. ISBN 0-87975-726-4. Order from Prometheus Press or any bookstore.

Unhooked: Staying Sober and Drug Free, by James Christopher 184 pages, $15.95. Prometheus Press, N.Y. 1989. ISBN 0-87975-564-4. Order from Prometheus Press or any bookstore.

How to Stay Sober: Recovery Without Religion, by James Christopher. 191 pages, $15.95. Prometheus Press, N.Y. 1988. ISBN 0-87975-457-5. Order from Prometheus Press or any bookstore.

LifeRing S.R. Brochures:

Sobriety Is Our Priority. When nothing works any more to control your drinking/using, try something new and radical: abstinence.

Secular Is Our Middle Name. What does 'secular' mean and what does it have to do with recovery?

Self-Help Is What We Do. To get clean and sober, and stay that way, empower your sober self.

The unhooked.com brochure. Describes www.unhooked.com, the general web site of LifeRing Secular Recovery.

All You Need Is Determination And a Computer.
Describes resources available for convenors of LifeRing
Secular Recovery Meetings.

*(All brochures are standard trifold format, available in
bundles of 50 at $5.00 & s/h from LifeRing Press; samples on
request)*

*LifeRing Press
1440 Broadway Suite 1000W
Oakland, CA 94612-2029
www.lifering.com books@lifering.com
Tel: 510-763-0779 Fax 510-763-1513*

*Order online, by phone or fax, or use
order blank on next page*

[Notes]

LifeRing Press Order Form

Qty	Title	Each	Extd
	Handbook of Secular Recovery. Book.	**$5.00**	
	Keepers: Voices of Secular Recovery. Book.	**$12.00***	
	My Personal Recovery Program: A Workbook. Forthcoming	**Call**	
	The Secular Prisoner Book. Forthcoming	**Call**	
	Sobriety Is Our Priority. Brochure. Bundle of 50.	**$5.00**	
	Secular Is Our Middle Name. Brochure. Bundle of 50.	**$5.00**	
	Self-Help Is What We Do. Brochure. Bundle of 50.	**$5.00**	
	The unhooked.com brochure. Bundle of 50. Free with order of two books and/or 3 brochure bundles.		
	All You Need Is Determination And a Computer. Brochure. Single copies only, free with any order.		
California **sales tax**, for all shipments to addresses in CA, add 8.25%			
Shipping, Priority Mail, for quantities of up to four Handbooks or six Keepers, or three brochure bundles, each package $4.00. Delivery within 3 days of shipment. Larger orders will be sent Standard Rate (books); delivery in about 8 days of shipment.			
		Total:	
Terms: check or MO with your order or we will ship and send you an invoice due and payable on receipt. (Sorry, no credit card orders.)			
*Call for meeting and institutional discounts on Keepers, or consult www.lifering.com for details			

Continued on next page

Please send books and invoice to:	
Name	
Title	
Firm	
Street	
City	
State	
Zip	
Phone	
Email	

If you want the books shipped to a different address, write it here:

LifeRing Press
1440 Broadway Suite 1000
Oakland, CA 94612-2029
www.lifering.com books@lifering.com
Tel: 510-763-0779
Fax 510-763-1513

LifeRing Press Order Form

Qty	Title	Each	Extd
	Handbook of Secular Recovery. Book.	**$5.00**	
	Keepers: Voices of Secular Recovery. Book.	**$12.00***	
	My Personal Recovery Program: A Workbook. Forthcoming	**Call**	
	The Secular Prisoner Book. Forthcoming	**Call**	
	Sobriety Is Our Priority. Brochure. Bundle of 50.	**$5.00**	
	Secular Is Our Middle Name. Brochure. Bundle of 50.	**$5.00**	
	Self-Help Is What We Do. Brochure. Bundle of 50.	**$5.00**	
	The unhooked.com brochure. Bundle of 50. Free with order of two books and/or 3 brochure bundles.		
	All You Need Is Determination And a Computer. Brochure. Single copies only, free with any order.		
California **sales tax**, for all shipments to addresses in CA, add 8.25%			
Shipping, Priority Mail, for quantities of up to four Handbooks or six Keepers, or three brochure bundles, each package $4.00. Delivery within 3 days of shipment. Larger orders will be sent Standard Rate (books); delivery in about 8 days of shipment.			
Total: Terms: check or MO with your order or we will ship and send you an invoice due and payable on receipt. (Sorry, no credit card orders.)			
Call for meeting and institutional discounts on Keepers, or consult www.lifering.com for details			

Please send books and invoice to:	
Name	
Title	
Firm	
Street	
City	
State	
Zip	
Phone	
Email	

If you want the books shipped to a different address, write it here:

LifeRing Press

1440 Broadway Suite 1000
Oakland, CA 94612-2029
www.lifering.com books@lifering.com
Tel: 510-763-0779
Fax 510-763-1513

Coming soon from LifeRing Press:

My Personal Recovery Program:
A Workbook

From the Introduction:
"Effective Treatment is individualized... The person who is best positioned to give the individual in recovery the kind of extended personalized therapeutic attention that is required for success is you, the individual in recovery."

Table of Contents (Condensed):
Introduction
Chapter 1.   My Decision
Chapter 2.   My Body
Chapter 3.   My Exposure
Chapter 4.   My Activities
Chapter 5.   My People
Chapter 6.   My Feelings
Chapter 7.   My Life Style
Chapter 8.   My Culture
Chapter 9.   My First Sober Life
Chapter 10. My Drinking/Using Career
Chapter 11. My Treatment And Support
             Group Experience
Chapter 12. About Relapse
Chapter 13. My Sober Day
Chapter 14. My Sober Week
Chapter 15. My Personal Recovery
             Program

Checklists – worksheets – essay topics – exercises for solo and group use

LifeRing Press
1440 Broadway Suite 1000W
Oakland, CA 94612-2029
www.lifering.com   books@lifering.com
Tel: 510-763-0779   Fax 510-763-1513